100

THINGS TO DO IN
CEDAR RAPIDS
BEFORE YOU
DIE

Wander across the Bridge of Lions
Photo courtesy of Cedar Rapids Tourism

100

THINGS TO DO IN
CEDAR RAPIDS
BEFORE YOU
DIE

KATIE MILLS GIORGIO

REEDY PRESS

Library of Congress Control Number: 2022936997

ISBN: 9781681063805

Design by Jill Halpin

All images are courtesy of the author or believed to be in the public domain unless otherwise noted.
Cover image: credit Calcam Ap
Back cover image: credit Jill Christine Photography

Printed in the United States of America
22 23 24 25 26   5 4 3 2 1

DEDICATION

For my family, the very best thing about Cedar Rapids.

CONTENTS

Preface xii

Acknowledgments xiv

Food and Drink

1. Have a Fancy Feast at Cobble Hill 2

2. Tantalize Your Tastebuds at NewBo City Market 3

3. Enjoy Cider and Sliders at Sutliff Farm and Cider House 4

4. Sample Iowa Wine and Spirits at Cedar Ridge Winery and Distillery.... 5

5. Grab a Brew at Lion Bridge Brewing Company 6

6. Eat Kolaches at Sykora Bakery 8

7. Celebrate Taco Tuesday at Caucho 9

8. Feast on Inventive Pizza at Fong's 10

9. Grab a Hot Dog at The Flying Wienie 11

10. Snag a Scoop at Dan and Debbie's Creamery 12

11. Start Your Day with a Sweet Treat at Donutland 13

12. Sling a Slice at Local Pizza Joints 14

13. Peek at Memorabilia at Irish Democrat 16

14. Eat a Pork Tenderloin as Big as Your Face at Joensy's........................ 17

15. Bite Into a Burrito at El Super Burrito & Lupita's Bakery 18

• •

16. Dine Among the Stacks at R.G. Books and Vino's Ristorante **20**

17. Give Back While Eating 'Cue at Willie Ray's Q Shack **21**

18. Order Up Some Seafood at Boston's **22**

19. Savor Wood-Fired Pizza at a Local Farm **24**

20. Savor Soul Food at Vivian's **26**

21. Enjoy a Class Act Meal at the Hotel at Kirkwood Center **28**

22. Toast a Bit of History at Little Bohemia **29**

23. Dine Overlooking Downtown at 350 First **30**

24. Gather with Friends at LP Street Food **31**

25. Fill Your Belly at Made-from-Scratch Cafés **32**

26. Enjoy Happy Hour at Upscale Restaurants **34**

27. Fill Your Mug at Local Coffee Shops **36**

28. Eat Your Way through Marion **38**

29. Share a Sweet Treat at Kava House & Café **40**

30. Buy Your Bread at Rustic Hearth Bakery **41**

31. Travel Back in Time at Lighthouse Inn Supper Club **42**

32. Dine Al Fresco at General Store Pub **43**

33. Eat on Main Street in Solon **44**

Music and Entertainment

34. Hear Symphony Music under the Stars at Brucemorchestra **48**

35. Hear World Music at CSPS **49**

● ●

36. Catch a Concert at McGrath Amphitheatre 50

37. Rock Out at Alliant Energy Powerhouse 51

38. Break a Leg at Theatre Cedar Rapids 52

39. Enjoy a Night on the Town at the Paramount Theatre 53

40. See a Ski Show on the Cedar River 54

41. Celebrate Independence at the Cedar Rapids Freedom Festival 56

42. Jive to Some Jazz at Jazz Under the Stars 57

43. Cozy Up at Giving Tree Theater 58

44. Play, Practice, and Party at Lowe Park 59

45. Explore Outer Space at Eastern Iowa Observatory 60

46. Spend a Day on the Farm at Wilson's Orchard 61

Sports and Recreation

47. Watch the Birds at Indian Creek Nature Center 64

48. Go Green in Greene Square Park 65

49. Pet Baby Animals at Old MacDonald's Farm 66

50. Conquer the Climb at Mount Trashmore Trails & Overlook 67

51. Catch a Fish at Prairie Park Fishery 68

52. Bike Around Town on Cedar Valley Trails 69

53. Cycle and Sip at Cedar Lake 70

54. Take a Tropical Escape at the Noelridge Greenhouses and Gardens.... 71

55. Snag a Trout at McLoud Run Stream 72

• •

56. Sink Your Putt at Twin Pines Golf Course **74**

57. Play with Nature at Wickiup Hill Outdoor Learning Center **75**

58. Find Peace at Prairiewoods Franciscan Spirituality Center **76**

59. Pick a Bushel of Apples at Allen's Orchard **77**

60. Camp Out at Pinicon Ridge Park **78**

61. Pick Out a Perfect Pumpkin at Local Pumpkin Patches **79**

62. Take a Walk through the Woods at Morgan Creek Park **80**

63. Make a Splash at Cherry Hill Pool and Park **81**

64. Get Rowdy at a Cedar Rapids Roughriders Hockey Game **82**

65. Cheer On the Boys of Summer at the Cedar Rapids Kernels **83**

66. Rev Your Engine at Hawkeye Downs **84**

67. Hike with a Llama at Prairie Patch Farm **85**

68. Hike the Bluffs at Palisades-Kepler State Park **86**

69. Say Boo at Bloomsbury Farm **87**

70. Brave the Waves at Manchester Whitewater Park **88**

71. Make Movie Dreams Come True at Field of Dreams **89**

72. Cut Your Own Bouquet at Local Flower Farms **90**

Culture and History

73. Immerse Yourself in Art at the Cedar Rapids Museum of Art **94**

74. Step into an Artist's Home at the Grant Wood Studio **95**

75. Look into Local History at the History Center **96**

76. Read a Book on the Roof at the Cedar Rapids Public Library.............. **97**

77. Honor Those Who Served Our Country
at Veterans Memorial Building.. **98**

78. Peep Public Art around Cedar Rapids.....................................**100**

79. Stop and Smell the Crunchberries at Quaker Oats................................**102**

80. Get in Touch with the History of Black Iowans
at the African American Museum of Iowa **103**

81. Check Out Czech and Slovak History
at the National Czech & Slovak Museum & Library **104**

82. Bring History to Life at Brucemore...**106**

83. Grab a Sarsaparilla Soda at Usher's Ferry Historic Village..................**108**

84. Invest in Art at the Marion Arts Festival **110**

85. Visit a Frank Lloyd Wright Home at Cedar Rock State Park **112**

86. Learn about the 31st President at the Herbert Hoover
Presidential Library and Museum...**113**

87. Eat and Shop Your Way through the Amana Colonies **114**

Shopping and Fashion

88. Find the Perfect Gift at SCOUT of Marion **118**

89. Invigorate Your Wardrobe at Local Women's Boutiques......................**120**

90. Toast the Town at 1st Avenue Wine House...**121**

91. Pick Up a Plant at Local Nurseries **122**

92. See and Be Seen at the Downtown Farmers Market **123**

• •

93. Add to Your Art Collection at Gilded Pear Gallery **124**

94. Snag a Snarky Tee at RAYGUN..**125**

95. Meet an Artist at Iowa Ceramics Center and Glass Studio **126**

96. Pick Up Your Next Read at Next Page Books.......................................**128**

97. Write Your Pen Pal at Scribe Stationer...**129**

98. Shop Small in the Czech Village **130**

99. Climb a Rock Wall at SOKO Outfitters..**132**

100. Experience Small Town Hospitality in Mount Vernon **133**

Activities by Season **134**

Suggested Itineraries **137**

Index **141**

PREFACE

"All I ever hope to say in books, all that I ever hope to say, is that I love the world."

—E.B. White

I love Cedar Rapids. I really do.

I was born here more than four decades ago. And while I've lived in other cities, this is where I've lived the longest, my hometown. It's where I've started a family of my own.

So, when I was asked if I'd be willing and able to come up with a list of 100 things that everyone who lives in or visits Cedar Rapids should do before they die, and write all about them, I jumped at the chance. You see, I love telling people about this place . . . all that is going on, what's new, and what you'd be surprised to know even if you've called this place home for a while.

This community has such a rich history, a vibrant present, and an exciting future. In my four decades alone, this city has flourished and changed so much. Cedar Rapids and I have grown up together . . . gotten cooler, or at least I like to think so.

In just the last couple of years, we've faced major natural disasters—most notably the flood of 2008 and the derecho of 2020—that brought hardship and destruction and changed the physical landscape of this place. But what we all learned during

• •

those heartbreaks and challenges is that the people who call Cedar Rapids home love this city very much and are willing to pick up the pieces to create an even better future.

This is a special place to call home. This is a destination worth visiting.

Cedar Rapids has long been called the City of Five Seasons, the fifth season being the time to enjoy the other four. After coming up with the list of things to do for this book (which is actually more than 100 things . . . you're welcome!), I decided that slogan is pretty fitting. I'll take all the time I can get in Cedar Rapids.

I hope after reading, you'll decide you'd like to make the most of your time in Cedar Rapids, too.

And I have to say I'm quite proud to hold proof in my hands to show to my teenage children, and the world, that there is in fact so much to do, see, and enjoy in Cedar Rapids, Iowa—more than 100 things, remember! And that puts a smile on my face. I hope as you read through and experience the things listed in this book, it puts a smile on yours, too. Maybe you can even add to the list!

Welcome to Cedar Rapids!

—Katie Mills Giorgio

ACKNOWLEDGMENTS

Writing this book is a true honor for this Cedar Rapidian. I would like to thank my extended network of friends both on and off Facebook who shared ideas—perhaps without knowing they would end up here in these pages—of their favorite things to do and places to eat, play, and shop around the Creative Corridor. People are awesome, and if you just ask, they are always ready to share about something they love. I would also like to thank Jennifer Pickar and the team at Cedar Rapids Tourism who have given me a reason to write about Cedar Rapids time and again over many years and even connected me with the opportunity to write this book. A big dose of gratitude for the whole team at Reedy Press for always answering my questions and so expertly and kindly guiding me through the process of bringing this book to life. I'm also thankful to all the people and organizations who so generously provided images to include within these pages. While it's fun to work magic with words, photography has a special way of drawing people in; this book would not be the same without it. Thank you, dear reader, for picking up this book for yourself or buying a copy for a friend. Books are very lonely things indeed if they only ever sit on a shelf. This one is very much written to be used as a guide, and I'm grateful you've given me a chance to share more than 100 things I've come to love about this city. Of course, last but certainly never least, I'd like to thank my family. They gave me suggestions for what to put "on the list" and had to listen to me brainstorm ideas while we drove around town or I sat at the kitchen table writing. You all continue to support me in whatever writing endeavor I take on. Thanks for being my favorite people to go on adventures with, even if only in our own backyard.

Grab tasty appetizers and beverages
at Lion Bridge Brewing Co.
Photo courtesy of Cedar Rapids Tourism

FOOD AND DRINK

HAVE A FANCY FEAST
AT COBBLE HILL

When Cobble Hill Eatery & Dispensary opened in Cedar Rapids back in 2013, the whole local dining scene in Cedar Rapids got a boost. In fact, it could be argued that your palate will never be more surprised and delighted than when you dine at Cobble Hill. With a New American menu and kitchen run by a James Beard Award Finalist, you know you are in for a fine dining treat. The creative menu changes seasonally, with a focus on sustainability and locally sourced foods. With each visit you can plan to enjoy an inventive starter, a delectable main course, and a deconstructed, mouth-watering dessert to finish the evening. Of course, the cocktail game is strong as well, so be sure to order something from the bar. The vintage chic vibe of the restaurant is a delight, making it a perfect spot for a special evening out. If you are able, snag a seat at the chef's table overlooking the kitchen and watch in wonder as dishes are prepared.

219 2nd St. SE, 319-366-3177
cobblehillrestaurant.com

TANTALIZE YOUR TASTEBUDS
AT NEWBO CITY MARKET

On any given weekend, you'll find the NewBo City Market abuzz with activity. Part small business incubator, part social food hall, and part community gathering space, NewBo City Market is a landmark and must-visit destination in the heart of the NewBo (short for New Bohemian) neighborhood. You'll find a variety of flavors to satisfy the tastebuds of every family member—from sweet treats to savory dishes—from the many shopkeepers preparing delectable foods. In addition, the NewBo bar serves up a selection of Iowa brews, and Roasters Coffee is always ready with a cup of Joe. There is also a teaching kitchen where guest chefs offer cooking classes for kids and adults. Several artisan start-ups also sell products within the converted warehouse space. During the summer months you'll find lots of outdoor activities, including farmers and artisans' markets, concerts, and yoga and other exercise classes taking place on the large market yard out front.

1100 3rd St. SE, 319-200-4050
newbocitymarket.org

ENJOY CIDER AND SLIDERS
AT SUTLIFF FARM AND CIDER HOUSE

One of Iowa's original cider producers, Sutliff Farm is the ideal place to sample their original hard cider or try a flavored cider or hard seltzer—the watermelon is spectacular. And while they are known for their adult beverages, don't miss out on a pulled pork sandwich slathered in barbecue sauce and served with a side of coleslaw. This restored homestead is a great pit stop if you are out on a long bike ride across the Iowa countryside, just took a hike at Palisades State Park, or are just heading home after a long day at the office. The barn houses the bar and restaurant, which opens from April through December on Thursdays through Sundays. It's a favorite spot for sipping a cool, crisp beverage while listening to live music in a classic Iowa setting.

382 Sutliff Rd., Lisbon, 319-535-0771
sutlifffarm.com

SAMPLE IOWA WINE AND SPIRITS
AT CEDAR RIDGE WINERY AND DISTILLERY

On a picturesque hill just south of Cedar Rapids in nearby Swisher you will find grapevines weaving along the landscape. While Iowa is known for growing corn and soybeans, the team at Cedar Ridge started producing Iowa-made wines back in 2005. They have since expanded and now offer a variety of sprits, including their award-winning bourbon whiskey—which has led the state of Iowa in sales for several years in a row. One secret is letting the whiskey age in non–temperature-controlled barrels, relying on Mother Nature to guide the process. The Cedar Ridge tasting room is a welcome pit stop. Plus, they play host to various events throughout the year, including live music and brunches. Snag a spot on the outdoor patio overlooking the vineyard while you sip on the Cedar Ridge lineup.

1441 Marak Rd., Swisher, 319-857-4300
crwine.com

GRAB A BREW
AT LION BRIDGE BREWING COMPANY

Lion Bridge Brewing Company has been a fixture in Czech Village for nearly a decade. The 10-barrel brewery offers the full gamut of beer styles, produced in small batches. They strive to craft approachable brews, but they also like to experiment. Compensation, an English mild ale, is perhaps their most popular beer and is always served on tap. They also offer an ever-changing list of specialty brews that they release seasonally, full of interesting flavors thanks to the brewers' creative use of spices, fruits, and herbs or local community collaborations. Find a spot to sit outdoors in the courtyard for a fun afternoon of sipping. You'll have a front row seat to all the activity of shoppers passing by in Czech Village. The brewery's menu should not be overlooked, either. Grab an order of the pierogies and the pretzels to snack on or stay for dinner.

59 16th Ave. SW, 319-200-4460
lionbridgebrewing.com

DESIGN YOUR OWN BREW TOUR
WITH THESE CEDAR RAPIDS BREWERIES

Iowa Brewing Company
708 3rd St., SE, 319-366-2337
iowabrewing.beer

Clock House Brewing
600 1st St. SE, 319-200-4099
clockhousebrewing.com

The Quarter Barrel
616 2nd Ave. SE, 319-200-4140
thequarterbarrel.com

Third Base Brewery
500 Blairs Ferry Rd. NE, 319-378-9090
thirdbasebrew.com

House Divided Brewery
1620 Dows St., Ely, 319-848-4197
housedividedbrewery.com

BIT Brewery
26 4th St. N, Central City, 319-438-3100
bitbrew3.com

EAT KOLACHES
AT SYKORA BAKERY

Cedar Rapids has a rich Czech and Slovak history, as many immigrants found their way to the Midwest beginning in the 1850s and settled in the area. Some of their culinary specialties are still alive and well, particularly at Sykora Bakery. This historic eatery first opened in the early 1900s, when there was just a dirt street and wooden sidewalk out front. The kolaches—a traditional Czech yeast pastry filled with fruits or cheeses—are a must, as they have been serving them from this location for over 100 years. They have more than a dozen flavors to choose from. Sykora also makes bohemian rye bread and offers a full Czech, Moravian, and Slovak menu. Part museum, part deli, ice cream shop, pizza parlor, and restaurant, this place does it all when it comes to an authentic cultural culinary experience.

73 16th Ave. SW, 319-364-5271
touchofclassphoto.wixsite.com/sykora

CELEBRATE TACO TUESDAY
AT CAUCHO

This is not your average taco spot. Caucho, a sister restaurant to Cobble Hill, offers a wide variety of gourmet-style Mexican food served up in a restaurant space with an eclectic, urban vibe. Start your meal with a flight of salsas, guacamole, and the queso fundido. Tortillas are made in-house daily, and you can taste the difference. There are al pastor, veggie, carnitas, and pollo tacos on the menu, and they always have surprisingly delicious specials. The bar serves up a variety of margaritas, other craft cocktails, and cerveza. Don't be afraid to try the Mexican Ashtray. They have a lovely little back patio for dining al fresco when the weather is nice. This unique eatery is definitely a great spot for girls' night out.

1202 3rd St. SE, Suite 102, 319-200-2525
cauchorestaurant.com

FEAST ON INVENTIVE PIZZA
AT FONG'S

Fong's is a playful place that takes making great pizza seriously. You'll find flavors from East Asia mixed with more traditional western notions of pizza toppings. Fong's is the home of the original crab rangoon pizza, a perennial favorite, and offers a whole host of other creative pies. They offer distinctive themed specials each month as well. The unique appetizer list is a tasty place to start the meal. As impressive as the pizza options are, the list of concoctions Fong's has come up with on the drink menu will make your jaw drop. Served up in quirky mugs, the tiki drink selection is sure to make you smile and delight your tastebuds all at once. If you are looking for unique cuisine, Fong's delivers.

1006 3rd St. SE, 319-320-9992
fongspizza.com/cedarrapids-2

GRAB A HOT DOG
AT THE FLYING WIENIE

You'll know you've found The Flying Wienie when you spot a bright yellow airplane perched on top of a hot dog stand in the middle of the city. The specialty at The Flying Wienie, of course, is Italian beef Chicago hotdogs with all the fixings: mustard, dill spears, onion, tomatoes, relish, sprouts, peppers, and celery salt, or topped your own way. But that's not all they serve. You'll find an assortment of other Chicago-style favorites on the menu, including ribs, Italian sausage, hand-cut fries, gyros, and burgers. First opened in 1999, this quaint eatery is a fun spot to grab lunch and dine outside on the picnic tables. They also offer party packs if you are looking to be the life of the next party you are invited to.

103 8th Ave. SW, 319-861-3036
theflyingwienie.com

SNAG A SCOOP
AT DAN AND DEBBIE'S CREAMERY

When you are looking for a cool treat, head to Dan and Debbie's Creamery in Ely. This family-run shop offers ice cream by the scoop or pint. With 12 signature flavors and a regular list of seasonal additions, there's something to please every sweet tooth. There are plenty of other farm-fresh dairy products, straight from the family's nearby farm. Grab a bag of cheese curds—so fresh they'll squeak—or a gallon of cream-top chocolate milk. An especially fun feature of a visit to the creamery is the observation window, where you can watch the Dan and Debbie's team hard at work, making their delightful dairy products. A bonus if you live in the area: sign up for home delivery from the Dan and Debbie's milkman. During summer months, the creamery is a popular spot for those on the nearby bike trail. And also during summer months you can also snag a bouquet of fresh-cut flowers from the family's flower farm in the summer as well.

1600 Main St., Ely, 319-848-6455
dananddebbies.com

START YOUR DAY WITH A SWEET TREAT
AT DONUTLAND

If Cedar Rapids had a signature donut, it would come from Donutland. This classic donut shop first opened its doors in 1971 and has been a go-to spot for families ever since. We cannot say enough about how tasty the chocolate chip donuts are. Of course, blueberry, cherry, cherry chocolate chip, Dutch crumb, and sprinkle donuts are also wildly popular. Donutland is open daily until 2 p.m. (or until donuts sell out for the day), and you can also grab a fresh cup of coffee, muffins, and bagels. The classic dozen will set you back just $11. And now, with the Big 15, you can take home more than just a dozen donuts to share with your family. We dare you not to eat one as soon as you get in your vehicle.

4307 Center Point Rd. NE, 319-393-0735
thedonutland.com

SLING A SLICE
AT LOCAL PIZZA JOINTS

If you wanted to have pizza for dinner every night of the week, the Cedar Rapids restaurant scene could meet that demand. At Tomaso's grab the Mambo Combo (their version of a supreme pizza) with Detroit crust and crispy cheese baked right to the edge of the pan. Zoey's Pizza has such a following, you'll often find quite the wait for a table in the small eatery, but it's always worth it. The zookie—hot and fresh skillet cookie—is the perfect treat. At Need Pizza you can have fun creating your own toppings. Do not be afraid to try mashed potatoes on your pizza. Honest. And while the pizzas at Cappy's Pizzeria are great, their calzones are another fun menu option.

Tomaso's Pizza
3234 Center Point Rd. NE, 319-364-4313
1207 7th Ave., Marion, 319-377-6102
1061 N Center Point Rd., Hiawatha, 319-393-5160
tomasos4me.com

Zoey's
690 10th St., Marion, 319-377-2840
zoeyspizza.com

Need Pizza
207 2nd Ave. SE, 319-362-6333
needcr.com

Cappy's Pizzeria
7037 C Ave. NE, 319-826-2625
cappyspizzapie.com

PEEK AT MEMORABILIA
AT IRISH DEMOCRAT

The Irish Democrat has been a favorite of many Cedar Rapidians—and politicians passing through town—since opening in the early 1980s. The walls are filled with Irish and political memorabilia collected over the years. To add a bit of whimsy, the space is always decorated to the nines for every holiday, including the large moose head overlooking the bar. Whether stopping in to grab a few drinks with friends, or dinner with the family—make sure to share an order of the wontons and chicken fingers and sample Calla's Irish stew—this classic Irish pub is a friendly spot.

3207 1st Ave. SE, 319-364-9896
irishdemocrat.net

TIP

A cult favorite on the west side of town is Leonardo's Restaurant & Pizza. Dine in one of the classic red leather booths or grab your food to go from their convenient carry-out window. This neighborhood pub has been a fixture in Cedar Rapids for nearly seven decades, serving up great pizza and classic sandwiches. 2228 16th Ave. SW, 319-364-5537 leonardoscr.com

EAT A PORK TENDERLOIN AS BIG AS YOUR FACE
AT JOENSY'S

When dining in Iowa, you can often find pork on the menu. But at Joensy's, pork is the menu. Known for their breaded pork tenderloin, which they make fresh every day, Joensy's has been a household name around the Cedar Rapids area for decades. With locations in Cedar Rapids and Center Point, you can order up a pork tenderloin so large you'll hardly believe your eyes. The size of it compared to the bun is sure to give you a good chuckle. Of course, they offer a few topping variations—cheese, bacon, grilled onions, and even buffalo sauce—for their tenderloins, so feel free to mix it up. Joensy's is a great spot to pick up lunch—always ask about their daily special—and their hot sandwich options offer a hearty meal, which can be especially fulfilling during cooler months.

220 Franklin St., Center Point, 319-849-1789
2600 Wiley Blvd., 319-390-4288
joensys.com

BITE INTO A BURRITO
AT EL SUPER BURRITO
& LUPITA'S BAKERY

Venture to El Super Burrito, where you'll find some of the best burritos in the city. In fact, it's the home of the Burrito Ahogado—a burrito filled with your choice of meat and beans and then smothered in green salsa, guacamole, and sour cream and served on a sizzling hot plate. Or, if you are especially daring and can take the heat, try the burrito bombero. This authentic Mexican restaurant, which is particularly popular during the lunch hour, mixes traditional fare with street eats, and has a wide menu featuring gorditas, tamales—which typically sell out—and more. Don't forget to grab a Mexican pastry: churros, pan dulche, and flan are always available. If you are dining in, you can even have hot churros served with ice cream.

3300 Johnson Ave. NW, 319-366-1181
elsuperburritocedarrapids.com

OTHER MEXICAN RESTAURANTS TO TRY OUT

La Cantina Bar & Grill
5400 Edgewood Rd. NE, 319-393-0924
3217 7th Ave., Marion, 319-409-5582
lacantinabarandgrill.com

Lucita's Diner
1100 1st St. SW, 319-200-2199
facebook.com/lucitas-diner-920236751444634

Hacienda Las Glorias
4317 Center Point Rd. NE, 319-294-0082
715 1st Ave. SW, 319-363-7344
haciendalasglorias.com

Villa's Patio
5200 Fountains Dr. NE, 319-302-9292
433 7th Ave., Marion, 319-447-1101
villaspatiomarion.com

DINE AMONG THE STACKS
AT R.G. BOOKS
AND VINO'S RISTORANTE

Dimly lit, with an air of mystique, R.G. Books is as close to a speakeasy as you'll find in Cedar Rapids. With a vintage bar and several bookshelf-lined booths to cozy up in for a cocktail or nightcap, this longtime Cedar Rapids drinking establishment is a favorite of those who know about it. The bar menu has an especially impressive list of craft cocktails and martinis. Try the Blue Goose, Prosecco di Pama, or the Ruby Red Pearl. And the adjoining restaurant, Vino's, is perhaps the best Italian restaurant in town, with savory steaks, succulent seafood, traditional and flavorful pasta dishes, and fine wines. It's a prime spot for a romantic celebratory meal. Tucked away into a suburban strip mall, R.G. Books and Vino's Ristorante are two Cedar Rapids gems that are sure to surprise and delight first-time visitors.

3611 1st Ave. SE, 319-363-7550
vinosristorante.com

GIVE BACK WHILE EATING 'CUE
AT WILLIE RAY'S Q SHACK

Willie Ray first made a name for himself by serving up mouth-watering barbecue from a tiny drive-through location on Cedar Rapids's northeast side. If you didn't know where it was located, you'd likely drive right on by. Owner Willie Ray Fairley was born and raised in Mississippi and blends his notion of hospitality with smoking meat—brisket, ribs, and chicken—to create an impressive and drool-worthy menu. The 'cue is available daily until sold out. But Willie Ray doesn't just stop at offering up incredible smoked meats. Any time a disaster strikes, whether in his own backyard or halfway across the country, Willie Ray gathers donations, loads up his barbecue grills, and heads out to offer food to those in need. With an incredibly giving owner, Willie Ray's Q Shack has become an example for the whole community of what caring for your neighbor looks, and tastes, like.

288 Blairs Ferry Rd. NE, 319-206-3806
willieraysqshack.com

ORDER UP
SOME SEAFOOD
AT BOSTON'S

Sure, Iowa is a landlocked state. But that doesn't mean you can't have a craving for seafood. Luckily, local restaurant Boston's dishes up fried fish and other seafood favorites that practically melt in your mouth. This longtime Cedar Rapids restaurant—and former fresh seafood market—was recently sold and remodeled, but it has stayed true to its seafood roots. The South End Crab Dip and Hush Puppies are the perfect place to start. There are several mac and cheese dishes to choose from. If you are feeling daring, try the crazy Cajun cod, which is served with a little kick. There are also walleye, catfish, shrimp, and salmon dishes to choose from. Of course, the fish and chips are a go-to order, especially popular for dine in or curbside pick-up during the Lenten season.

804 5th St. SE, 319-363-9627
bostonscr.com

TIP

Boston's has several sister restaurants around Cedar Rapids, including Midtown Station, located right across the street from the city's Central Fire Station, and Tic Toc, a long-standing neighborhood eatery that recently got a major overhaul. Both serve breakfast, lunch, and dinner and have some irresistible dishes that you simply must try. Midtown serves all-day breakfast and has delicious Brussel sprouts. Tic Toc has giant mozzarella sticks and greasy good onion rings.

Midtown Station
715 2nd Ave. SE, 319-200-1094
midtownstationcr.com

Tic Toc
600 17th St. NE, 319-200-4210
tictoccr.com

SAVOR WOOD-FIRED PIZZA
AT A LOCAL FARM

Pizza has never tasted better than when it's pulled straight from a wood-fired oven. Several small Iowa farms just outside of Cedar Rapids take this concept up a notch. Guests are invited to head out to the farm and enjoy a slice (or two) of hot, homemade pizza in the evening light of summer. With fresh ingredients and sometimes surprising toppings (have you ever tried a triple berry pizza?) the pizzas will delight your tastebuds while you watch the fireflies come out to play. Pizza lovers should plan to bring their own chairs or a blanket for the lawn. Luna Valley Farm also offers overnight glamping accommodations, but they book up quickly each season.

Stone Wall Pizza
3297 320th St., Wellman, 319-530-3239
stonewallpizza.com

Luna Valley Farm
3012 Middle Sattre Rd., Decorah
lunavalleyfarm.com

SAVOR SOUL FOOD
AT VIVIAN'S

Iowa is definitely a Midwestern state, but thanks to Vivian's Soul Food, Cedar Rapidians can get a little taste of Southern hospitality nearly any day of the week. With a mission to bring people together through soul food, Vivian's dishes up their flavorful, homemade dishes for lunch, dinner, and special catering events. Known for their fried chicken, seasoned collard greens, and baked mac and cheese, this eatery also offers up jerk chicken, fried okra, and chicken and waffles. It's a menu with a strong, flavorful influence you aren't likely to find elsewhere in town. Every visit offers up a helping of comfort food and a field trip for your taste buds. And the customer service will have you feeling like family.

2925 Williams Pkwy. SW, 319-396-2229
vivianssoulfoodcr.com

OTHER HIDDEN GEMS
THAT OFFER GLOBAL FLAVORS

Siamville Thai Cuisine
3635 1st Ave. SE, 319-364-1955
siamville.com

Phong Lan Vietnamese Restaurant
216 8th St. SE, 319-365-5784

Persis Biryani Indian Grill
4862 1st Ave. NE, 319-826-2000
persiscedarrapids.com

Tee's Liberian Dish
1271 1st Ave. SE, 609-516-4427
teesliberiandish.com

ENJOY A CLASS ACT MEAL
AT THE HOTEL AT KIRKWOOD CENTER

Guests of the Hotel at Kirkwood Center, located on the outskirts of town near the airport, are lucky enough to find this restaurant just off the main lobby. But The Class Act is open to the public for fine dining as well. It's a great spot for a romantic night out, a family celebration, or a business meeting. With entrees ranging from seared duck breast and grilled ribeye to fried eggplant, the dining experience is a treat, especially if you don't skip dessert. Interestingly, the restaurant also provides real-time teaching experience for Kirkwood Community College's Culinary Arts program. The restaurant, and the whole hotel in fact, are the only teaching hotel in the country where the staff is actively working to hone their service industry skills.

7725 Kirkwood Blvd. SW, 319-848-8700
thehotelatkirkwood.com/the-class-act-restaurant.htm

TOAST A BIT OF HISTORY
AT LITTLE BOHEMIA

Known to the locals as Little Bo's, this tavern on the corner in the heart of the NewBo neighborhood is the perfect spot to belly up to the bar and drink in a little history lesson. At one time it was a known hangout of famed Cedar Rapids artist Grant Wood and his lesser-known but incredibly talented friend Marvin Cone (who created a now-well-known painting of the bar in 1941). Little Bohemia has been a favorite spot of the creative and working classes for decades. In fact, Little Bo's is the oldest tavern in town, serving cold beverages since 1934. The building went up in the 1880s! Little Bo's also serves up some tasty bar food, including a popular pork tenderloin (breaded and fried to order), and the bartenders make a mean margarita. The walls are lined from floor to ceiling with old advertising signs, photos, and knick-knacks, each with a story of its own.

1317 3rd St. SE, 319-366-6262

DINE OVERLOOKING DOWNTOWN
AT 350 FIRST

If you like to dine in a room with a view, head on up to 350 First. This restaurant is situated at the top of the DoubleTree Hotel in downtown Cedar Rapids. Sixteen floors up you can take in the matrix of downtown (especially fun with the city lights at night) or look out over the Cedar River. And it's not just the views that are impressive. The menu, which changes slightly for each season, offers great sandwiches and truffle fries along with delectable seafood, vegetarian, and steak entrees. The signature salad is a delightful option for those looking for a lighter meal. And those signature DoubleTree Hotel cookies make a menu appearance in the form of a dessert sundae. There is often live music in the lounge area as well, making it a fun spot if you only want to grab drinks at the highest possible elevation in CR.

350 1st Ave. NE, 319-731-4483
facebook.com/CR350First

GATHER WITH FRIENDS
AT LP STREET FOOD

LP Street Food in the Kingston Village neighborhood believes having fun is more important than being fancy. The restaurant invites patrons to stop for their "fresh twist on culturally rich, gastronomically delightful street food." The menu is inspired by food trucks and walk-up windows around the country, running the gamut from gyros, ramen, and corn dogs to poutine, cheesesteak, and more. And don't pass up their fruity libations, either. The restaurant itself gives off a playful, welcoming vibe. The interior of the space was designed using pieces rescued from old barns, churches, and junkyards to give it an eclectic feel. The large outdoor patio is an especially fun spot in warm-weather months, whether you are biking through town or need a gathering place for a group. And their recent addition of patio igloos allows those up for a unique dining experience to enjoy one any time of the year.

302 3rd Ave. SW, 319-364-4042
lpstreetfood.com

TIP
In warm-weather months, grab some ice cream from the LP Scoop Coop on the outdoor patio.

FILL YOUR BELLY
AT MADE-FROM-SCRATCH CAFÉS

If you grew up with a grandmother who made pasta and pies from scratch, you can appreciate the love and time that goes into a meal. Several restaurants around town take those lessons to heart, offering visitors a taste of a made-from-scratch approach to eating out. Feedwell Kitchen & Bakery is a partnership between two friends, one of whom loves to cook and one of whom loves to bake. The result is a delightful café serving fresh meals for breakfast and lunch. At Lightworks Café you can not only grab an artfully poured coffee, but also snag made-from-scratch lunch items and grab-and-go pre-made meals for home. Don't miss out on their potpies. And at Groundswell Café you can not only enjoy a delicious meal for breakfast or lunch yourself—including an omelet, sandwich, wrap, or salad and soup—but also pay it forward, leaving money in the community jar for someone who might not be able to afford to pay for their meal. It's food that feels good and tastes good.

Feedwell Kitchen & Bakery
560 Boyson Rd., 319-409-6905
feedwellkitchenandbakery.com

Lightworks Café
501 7th Ave. SE, Ste. B, 319-449-4046
lightworkscafe.com

Groundswell Café
201 3rd Ave. SW, 319-362-2214
groundswell.hub25.org

ENJOY HAPPY HOUR
AT UPSCALE RESTAURANTS

Sometimes you just need a lovely place to sip a fancy cocktail. While these eateries are upscale, they are also approachable, making them a prime spot to meet up with co-workers or friends during happy hour. They are fantastic spots for both food and drinks. Downtown, try Black Sheep Social Club, where they have 24 beers on tap—focusing on local brews—and come up with cocktails inspired by the kitchen and the garden. Head to Czech Village and belly up to the bar at rodina. Here, meals are inspired by family-style dining and the drinks are inventive, yet well balanced. They have options if you are looking for smoky, sweet, or anything in between and are happy to mix up a mocktail as well. On the northeast side of town, Zeppelins is another prime spot known for its two-for-one specials on all drinks from 3 p.m. to 6 p.m. every day. Their appetizers are also stellar—try the wontons, the parmesan fries, and the fire-roasted corn queso.

Black Sheep Social Club
600 1st St. SE, 319-200-7070
iamtheblacksheep.com

rodina
1507 C St. SW, 319-200-2515
rodinaiowa.com

Zeppelins
5300 Edgewood Rd. NE, 319-393-3047
zeppelinscr.com

FILL YOUR MUG
AT LOCAL COFFEE SHOPS

So many coffee shops, so little time. Lucky for espresso lovers, the Cedar Rapids area boasts an impressive number of locally owned spots to grab a cup of joe, have a tasty breakfast treat, and catch up with friends. Each shop has its own ambience. Some are in older, rustic buildings with lots of space to spread out. Others are in newer buildings with comfy couches for curling up. A few spots, including Café St. Pio, Brewhemia, and Dash Coffee Roasters offer more robust breakfast and lunch menus as well. Kismet is both a coffee house and a flower shop. Stillwater Coffee Co. hosts live music and morning yoga. So, pop into each spot to find your local coffee shop match.

Craft'd
333 1st St. SE, 319-261-4901
facebook.com/craftdcr

Café St. Pio
99 16th Ave. SW, 319-200-1000
cafe-saint-pio.business.site

Brewhemia
1202 3rd St. SE, 319-364-0802
brewhemia.com

Stillwater Coffee Co.
1275 N Center Point Rd., Hiawatha, 319-200-2739
stillwatercoffeeco.com

Dash Coffee Roasters
120 3rd Ave. SW, 319-423-9297
dashcoffeeroasters.com

Kismet Coffee & Bloom
1000 3rd St. SE, 319-200-3218
kismetcoffeebloom.com

Mr. Beans
1080 E Post Rd., Marion, 319-826-3929
annarizer.wixsite.com/marionmrbeans

EAT YOUR WAY
THROUGH MARION

In the last couple of years, Marion restaurants have really put the city on the dining map. When you are looking for a cool vibe, pop into the hip-stir to dine in a barrel booth and enjoy eclectic, trendy, unexpected dishes. Goldfinch Tap + Eatery is the perfect spot for enjoying Midwest classic dishes made from scratch. The large outdoor patio is a fun dining spot. Short's Burgers & Shine, not surprisingly, offers up some great burger selections, more than 20 on one menu. And when you need a ridiculously sweet treat, head to Frydae, where they concoct loaded ice cream shakes and sundaes. The street fries—choose from waffle, straight cut, or sweet potato and a whole host of toppings—can satisfy any salty cravings.

the hip-stir
1120 7th Ave., Marion, 319-200-5465
facebook.com/thehipstir

Goldfinch Tap + Eatery
740 10th St., Marion, 319-826-2047
goldfinchtap.com

Short's Burgers & Shine
780 11th St., Marion, 319-200-1020
marion.shortsburger.com

Frydae
743 10th St., Marion, 319-200-4550
finallyfrydae.com

SHARE A SWEET TREAT
AT KAVA HOUSE & CAFÉ

Kava House & Café in Swisher welcomes patrons into a former general store that dates to 1914. The cozy, country atmosphere gives this restaurant a welcoming and down-home feel. Kava House is a wonderful spot to meet a friend for breakfast. They open at 6:30 a.m. on weekdays (8 a.m. on Saturdays, closed Sunday and Monday) so it's a nice spot to grab a coffee if you are out the door early. Be sure to also select a bakery treat as well: a fresh scone, cinnamon roll, muffin, bread pudding, coffee cake, or kolache. They also serve hot breakfast casseroles. Kava House does lunch and dinner as well, offering sandwiches, salads, and a daily homemade soup. On Friday nights, stop by to grab a Kava burger (with eight varieties to choose from) or on Saturday evening call ahead to see what the dinner special for the evening is. But truly, it's the dessert counter at Kava House that cannot be beat. The very generous slices of red velvet cake, carrot cake, mint brownies, salted nut roll bars, pumpkin bars, rice krispie treats, and more are all decadent treats.

122 2nd St. SE, Swisher, 319-857-5000
kavahousecafe.com

BUY YOUR BREAD
AT RUSTIC HEARTH BAKERY

If you have a love affair with bread, make sure you visit Rustic Hearth Bakery on the Cedar Rapids's southeast side. Recently voted the best bread in Iowa—yes, the whole state!—this bakery got its start in NewBo City Market several years ago before branching out into its own retail storefront. Rustic Hearth Bakery got a jump on the sourdough craze of 2020. Sourdough breads have long been the bakery's specialty, hand crafted the old-fashioned way and made with locally sourced ingredients. On any given day, a visit to the bakery will reveal several varieties of sourdough available, including rustic, rye, seeded, and whole wheat. They also offer a monthly rotating flavored sourdough. You can also take home baguettes, pretzel rolls, pecan rolls, croissants, cookies, muffins, and more.

3531 Mount Vernon Rd. SE, 319-200-4008
rustichearthbakery.com

TRAVEL BACK IN TIME
AT LIGHTHOUSE INN SUPPER CLUB

Years ago, travelers took to Highway 30 to travel between Chicago and the Cedar Rapids area. Supper clubs dotted the highway so weary travelers could grab a meal or find a place to stay for the night. The Lighthouse Inn and Supper Club opened in 1912 and was a pit stop favored by many over the last century. Rumor has it that Al Capone, John Dillinger, and other Chicago mobsters dined here during the Prohibition era. Today, the Lighthouse Inn and Supper Club is still standing and serving up hearty meals to travelers from near and far. While there's no longer an inn, this roadside restaurant is still a favorite of many. It's known for barbecued ribs, broasted chicken, steak, and seafood, so you'll leave the Lighthouse Inn with a full belly. Do make sure to also pop into Josie's Dive to grab a night cap.

6905 Mount Vernon Rd. SE, 319-362-3467
crlighthouseinn.com

DINE AL FRESCO
AT GENERAL STORE PUB

Take a drive through Grant Wood country. Famed artist Grant Wood grew up on a farm in Jones County, just to the east of Cedar Rapids. As you drive the rolling countryside, you'll see why and how the beautiful landscape informed the work of Grant Wood. You can even make your way through Stone City, where Wood and friends once had an artists' colony. Nearby, make a pit stop at General Store Pub. This old, limestone building was built in 1897 and is featured in one of Grant Wood's paintings. Once the town's general store, it has since been converted into a bar and restaurant. Try the tacklebox appetizer sampler, a Wapsi-Rita from the bar, or the TAD burger (topped with cheese, bacon, and a fried egg). The pub is situated right on the banks of the Wapsipinicon River, and the large outdoor deck has some of the best seats in the house. There's often live musical entertainment as well.

12612 Stone City Rd., Anamosa, 319-462-4399
generalstorepub.com

EAT ON MAIN STREET
IN SOLON

Solon is just a short drive or bike ride south of Cedar Rapids and near to Lake McBride, which is a fun spot to spend a day in the sun. If you are in the area in the morning, pop into The Eat Shop. A relative newcomer on the culinary scene, this boutique bake shop has a rich history of whipping up delightful treats for patrons in the area. Everything is made from scratch, and people can't stop raving about the cinnamon rolls. Just across the street is Big Grove Brewpub. An extension of the brewery located in nearby Iowa City, this restaurant and bar offers up delicious apps, entrees, and tasty brews, and has an impressive courtyard for outdoor dining for lunch and dinner.

TIP
Once you've filled your belly, pop into MOXIE + mortar. The home décor store has fun finds to cozy up your interior spaces and also offers wine tasting.

The Eat Shop
120 W Main St. #1, Solon, 319-624-2014
theeatshop.com

Big Grove Brewpub
100 W Main St., Solon, 319-624-2337
biggrove.com/solon-brewpub

MOXIE + mortar
121 W Main St., Solon, 319-624-2829
moxieandmortar.com

Take in the majesty of the Paramount Theater in downtown.
Photo courtesy of Cedar Rapids Tourism

MUSIC
AND ENTERTAINMENT

HEAR SYMPHONY MUSIC UNDER THE STARS
AT BRUCEMORCHESTRA

If you have the biggest front yard in the city, you might as well host a party. That's exactly what the team at Brucemore does when they partner with Orchestra Iowa to present Brucemorchestra. Join thousands of music lovers as Orchestra Iowa sets up a large outdoor stage on the expansive, natural sloping front lawn at the Brucemore mansion. They perform a well-known symphony— the selection changes each year and usually appeals to avid symphony attendees as well as newbies—as guests kick back in lawn chairs or laze on blankets. Many people pack a picnic charcuterie and bring a bottle of wine, or two, to make for a special evening under the stars. The show happens each fall and is typically the kickoff to Orchestra Iowa's upcoming season.

2160 Linden Dr. SE, 319-366-8203
artsiowa.com/orchestra

HEAR WORLD MUSIC
AT CSPS

CSPS is the kind of venue where you come to discover something new. In this unique, historic setting, some 100 eclectic musical and theater acts from all around the world—many touring for the first time in Cedar Rapids—perform each year. There is also a black box theater and several gallery spaces within the building that showcase works by local, regional, national, and international artists in anywhere from 15 to 20 exhibitions a year. The building was home to a Czech fraternal club more than 100 years ago and has played host to many community gatherings and dances over the decades. It was historically preserved after the flood of 2008 and is now a hub of activity in the NewBo neighborhood housing several retail businesses on the first floor. During open hours and concerts, you can grab a drink at Carlo, the second-floor bar, and marvel at the beauty and history of the building.

1103 3rd St. SE, 319-364-1580
cspshall.org

CATCH A CONCERT
AT MCGRATH AMPHITHEATRE

If you are a fan of live music, then you've got to take in a concert at McGrath Amphitheatre. This outdoor setting right on the west bank of the Cedar River is a fun spot with a casual concert vibe. It's hosted everything from community events and local bands to national touring comedy acts, country crooners, and music legends. The lawn seating makes for a venue where there's not a bad seat in the "house." Some shows have reserved seating, while others allow guests to bring their own lawn chair. It's a prime spot for enjoying a concert in the summer months. While parking is not ideal in the neighborhood, the amphitheater is just a short walk from many downtown eateries where you can grab drinks or a quick bite before the show.

475 1st St. SW, 319-362-1729
creventslive.com/p/venues/mcgrathamphitheatre

ROCK OUT
AT ALLIANT ENERGY POWERHOUSE

The Powerhouse is rocking! Formerly called the US Cellular Center and the Five Seasons Center, this large venue—with some 9,000 seats—has been an entertainment hub in the Cedar Rapids area for decades. The first concert that was held in the arena when it opened in 1979 was the English rock band Yes. Throughout the year, this arena, located in the heart of downtown, plays host to a variety of entertainment events, including major touring musical artists and productions, monster truck jams, rodeos, and sporting events. A 2013 renovation added the adjoining convention center that now hosts numerous community activities, including conferences, fundraisers, and large expos like Comic Con. It is also connected to the DoubleTree Hotel, which is convenient if you need an overnight stay.

370 1st Ave. NE, 319-398-5211
creventslive.com/alliantenergypowerhouse

BREAK A LEG
AT THEATRE CEDAR RAPIDS

Local theater has been alive and well in Cedar Rapids since the 1920s. Today, Theatre Cedar Rapids, in the historic Iowa Theater Building, keeps the tradition alive. And thanks to the talent you'll see displayed on stage, you will be stunned to know it's a community theater production. In fact, Theatre Cedar Rapids is one of the largest professionally run volunteer theater organizations in the country. There are typically nine productions each year on the main stage, ranging from classic musical theater to more contemporary plays. Ensemble casts delight audience members young and old. There is also an intimate black box theater in the basement of the building. And the Linge Lounge offers signature drinks—developed to complement each production—to enjoy before or after the show.

102 3rd St. SE, 319-366-8591
theatrecr.org

ENJOY A NIGHT ON THE TOWN
AT THE PARAMOUNT THEATRE

There's nothing like listening to an artistic performance while sitting in a space that is a work of art in its own right. That's the experience you'll get when you attend a show at the Paramount Theatre in downtown Cedar Rapids. This historic theater, which opened in 1928 and was fully restored after the devastating flood of 2008, is a stunning work of architecture, with a sparkling glass grand lobby and intricate decorative details at every turn. Whether you are taking in a performance of Orchestra Iowa— Cedar Rapids's premiere 68-person orchestra that offers classical, ballet, opera, popular, and chamber performances throughout the year and calls the theater home—or you are seeing a touring Broadway production or live concert event, every visit to the Paramount Theatre is a memorable one.

123 3rd Ave. SE, 319-366-8203
creventslive.com/p/venues/paramounttheatre

TIP
Cedar Rapids Opera Theater presents two or three operas each season, often at the Paramount Theatre. These high-caliber productions are a great introduction to the opera. 319-365-7401, cropera.org

SEE A SKI SHOW
ON THE CEDAR RIVER

When a river runs through the center of your city, you'd better believe there will be some entertainment opportunities related to the showpiece waterway. Enter the Five Seasons Ski Team. Every Thursday night during summer months, you'll find this club putting together a spectacular show on the river at Ellis Park. Each year the show has a different theme and includes graceful ballet moves, daredevil jumps, towering pyramids, and even high-speed barefoot skiing. You'll be amazed at what this group of nearly 100 water-skiing enthusiasts can do. Their free performance is sure to amaze the whole family. Some bleacher seating is available, but it does fill up fast, so you are welcome to bring your own chair or blanket to sit on. Five Season Ski Team members will tell you the most important thing to bring along is a loud cheering voice.

2021 Ellis Blvd. NW, 319-804-8754
5sst.com

TIP

Arrive a bit early to not only grab a prime viewing spot for the show, but also enjoy a picnic dinner. The Shakespeare Garden, a hidden gem just across the street in Ellis Park, is a lovely spot to dine al fresco.

916 Ellis Blvd. NW

CELEBRATE INDEPENDENCE
AT THE CEDAR RAPIDS FREEDOM FESTIVAL

One day is not enough to celebrate freedom. So, each year, the Cedar Rapids community takes a couple of weeks to celebrate our nation's independence leading up to the 4th of July. Since 1988, the Freedom Festival has been organizing lots of patriotic fun. Events take place in every quadrant of the city for residents and visitors of all ages to enjoy. Favorites include the annual 4th of July road race, a pancake breakfast, a parade, the Dock Dogs jumping contest, the Balloon Glow, and several musical concerts. Snag a Freedom Festival button for the chance to win prizes and enjoy discounts or admittance to the events. Of course, the evening of the 4th is capped off with a spectacular fireworks display set off from the heart of downtown.

319-365-8313
freedomfestival.com

JIVE TO SOME JAZZ
AT JAZZ UNDER THE STARS

Cedar Rapids's local jazz station, KCCK-FM—found at 88.3 on your radio—hosts a series of outdoor concerts each August to bring the cool skits and skats of jazz bands to a parklike setting. These free events are opportunities for residents and visitors alike to pack up a picnic dinner—or plan to grab something from the local food trucks that set up for the event—and their comfiest lawn chairs and blankets and spend a night relaxing under the stars while musicians jive away. Dancing is certainly encouraged if the music moves you. The concerts are also broadcast live on KCCK for those who can't make it to the park for the evening.

4900 Council St. NE, 319-398-5446
kcck.org/juts

TIP

If you really enjoy outdoor concerts, be sure to check out the schedule for the Cedar Rapids Municipal Band, which plays in various parks throughout the summer months. Brucemore's Music in the Courtyard is another unique opportunity to take in some tunes in a dreamy, starry setting.

COZY UP
AT GIVING TREE THEATER

If you like your theatrical experiences up close and personal, then head over to Giving Tree Theater. This small, black box–style theater located in Marion offers one of the most intimate live theater experiences in the area. Attendees pick a cozy seat on vintage couches and chairs—that may in fact look just like one your grandmother used to have. You'll be as comfy as you would be in your own living room as you sit just a few feet from the stage and watch volunteer actors bring a story to life. Don't forget to grab some popcorn and a local brew before the show begins. Another community theater initiative, Giving Tree Theater is also distinct in that each production identifies a local nonprofit that benefits from ticket sales for that particular show.

752 10th St., Marion, 319-536-0257
givingtreetheater.com

PLAY, PRACTICE, AND PARTY
AT LOWE PARK

Lowe Park is Marion's hub of outdoor activities, especially in warm-weather months. There's sunrise yoga on many Saturday mornings throughout the summer. The Klopfenstein Amphitheater, with a unique tree-inspired design, often hosts concerts and other community events for the whole family. Plus, there are several playgrounds for little ones to explore and baseball diamonds often busy with little league tournaments. There is a wonderful walking trail through the park and several large art installations to enjoy. The park is also home to the Lowe Park Arts and Environment Center, which always has an interesting selection of works by local artists and schoolchildren on display. Do also make time to wander through the Linn County Master Gardeners demonstration gardens and the children's discovery garden, where you'll see an amazing selection of flowers each summer to perhaps help inspire your own planting.

4500 N 10th St., Marion, 319-447-3590
cityofmarion.org/recreation/parks-recreation/lowe-park-amphitheater

EXPLORE OUTER SPACE
AT EASTERN IOWA OBSERVATORY

It's always easier to see the stars when you are outside the city. That's even more true when you make the short drive to the Eastern Iowa Observatory. Located just 15 minutes east of Cedar Rapids, this observatory is run by the Cedar Amateur Astronomers Club. Visitors can take part in regular public viewing sessions and programs to understand more about the night sky and the galaxies beyond. With two large-scale permanently mounted telescopes—one of which is known to be the largest telescope available for public use in the state—you'll even get a more than average glimpse into outer space. If your timing is right and the sky is clear, you might see the rings around Saturn. The volunteer astronomers are always happy to answer questions, which is reassuring if you sometimes have trouble even finding the big dipper.

1365 Ivanhoe Rd., Ely, 319-848-2068
cedar-astronomers.org/pal-dows-observatory

SPEND A DAY ON THE FARM
AT WILSON'S ORCHARD

Wilson's Orchard & Farm has earned a reputation over 40 years as the premiere apple orchard in the area. And while u-pick apples remain the main draw of the farm—pay attention to when the Honeycrisp apples are ready for plucking—in recent years, the owners have added a whole host of other activities to bring families out to enjoy the farm time and again. You can now pick strawberries, blueberries, peaches, pumpkins, flowers, and more; visit with farm animals; take a hayrack ride; and even go ice skating and sledding in the winter. You can pick up other goods—like hard and sweet cider and take-and-bake pies—at the farm market throughout the year. And you don't want to miss out on grabbing a meal at Wilson's Ciderhouse & Venue. This restaurant offers a seasonally changing menu inspired by foods grown on the farm and other local food partners and prepared by an award-winning chef. The views while you dine are picturesque and uniquely Iowan.

4823 Dingleberry Rd. NE, Iowa City, 319-354-5651
wilsonsorchard.com

Keep cool in Greene Square Park.
Photo courtesy of Cedar Rapids Tourism

SPORTS
AND RECREATION

WATCH THE BIRDS
AT INDIAN CREEK NATURE CENTER

Indian Creek Nature Center is arguably the best spot to get in touch with the great outdoors in the Cedar Rapids area. It's situated on more than 200 acres near where Indian Creek meets the Cedar Rapids, and there are wetlands, riparian forest, maple sugarbush, tallgrass prairies, and oak savannas to explore on myriad trails. The organization's mission is to create champions of nature in visitors young and old any time of the year. During the summer months you can enjoy outdoor yoga on the terrace or catch a concert in the forest amphitheater. If you're willing to get your feet wet, you can even stomp through the creek. During the winter you can borrow a pair of snowshoes to appreciate the beauty of the snow-covered landscape. A perennial favorite spot is the bird room inside the main Amazing Space building, where you can sit and observe the birds and other wildlife that frequent the Nature Center property. And don't miss the Maple Syrup Festival in the early spring.

5300 Otis Rd. SE, 319-362-0664
indiancreeknaturecenter.org

GO GREEN
IN GREENE SQUARE PARK

In the heart of Downtown Cedar Rapids, you will find Greene Square Park. Officially created in 1843, the park was once a hub for the city's train depot, which has long been torn down. Today, Greene Square Park is a hub of community gathering. Renovated in recent years to make the park more welcoming and a more flexible gathering space, it now features a large art installation, *Rolic* by California sculptor Bruce Beasley, that practically begs visitors young and old to crawl through it. Kids won't be able to resist the interactive water feature during warmer weather months either. During the holiday season, the park is decorated with the city's Christmas tree and a host of other festive lights. Situated between the Cedar Rapids Museum of Art and the Cedar Rapids Public Library, this city green space is a great spot to meet with friends or enjoy an event.

Corner of 3rd Street Southeast and 3rd Avenue Southeast
cedar-rapids.org/residents/parks_and_recreation/parks.php

PET BABY ANIMALS
AT OLD MACDONALD'S FARM

Old MacDonald's Farm is a longtime favorite spot for Cedar Rapids families and visitors. For more than 100 years it has offered a chance to get up close and personal with some friendly farm animals. Chickens, bunnies, turtles, ducks, goats, cattle, oh my! The kid-centric facility even hosts "farmer for a day" programs during the summer for little ones to get some firsthand experience caring for the animals. A visit to Old MacDonald's Farm—which is open from May through October—is always free, so it can be a nice spot for a visit whether you have five minutes or five hours to spare. It's located within Bever Park, one of the most popular parks on the city's southeast side, in a lovely historic neighborhood with towering, old oak trees.

2700 Bever Ave. SE, 319-286-5760
cedar-rapids.org/residents/parks_and_recreation/old_macdonald_s_farm.php

CONQUER THE CLIMB
AT MOUNT TRASHMORE
TRAILS & OVERLOOK

Claim your chance to experience the most unique outdoor adventure in the whole Midwest by hiking up a pile of trash. No kidding! The city's famed "Mount Trashmore" was in fact a former landfill site—filled with six million tons of trash—that has been transformed into a suburban recreation site. There are several trails that will take you to the top as you embark on the "Mount Trashmore Challenge." The unique gravity-fed flow trail is perfect for those interested in mountain biking. The Stumptown Trail is the longest, as it winds around the "mount," while the overlook trail is the most direct route to the top. Checking in at the recreation building—taking advantage of the hydration station— is required (because it's a regulated waste management site) before trekking or biking to the top. The panoramic view of the city from the top is like no other in the area and worth every step.

2250 A St. SW, 319-377-5290
solidwasteagency.org/mount-trashmore

CATCH A FISH
AT PRAIRIE PARK FISHERY

Anglers young and old will find Prairie Park Fishery, tucked away on the city's southeast side, to be a quiet spot for a morning of fishing. Most successfully fished by canoe, kayak, or rowboat—no motorized boats allowed here—the 65-acre lake at the center of the park is home to a variety of fish, including walleye, bluegill, large- and small-mouth bass, channel catfish, and others. The trail that runs around the lake is just under two miles long and also connects to the Sac and Fox Trail for those interested in biking to and from the site. Visitors to the park are also welcome to enjoy a picnic or to try geocaching or even scuba diving in the lake, which was formerly a quarry.

2125 Otis Rd. SE, 319-286-5760
cedar-rapids.org/residents/parks_and_recreation/prairie_park_fishery.php

---

TIP

If you are in the area during the winter months, keep your eyes peeled for bald eagles who frequent the large, bare trees along the banks of the Cedar River as they search for meals in the open water. At times, there can be several dozen eagles, which is a sight that I promise will stop you in your tracks.

BIKE AROUND TOWN
ON CEDAR VALLEY TRAILS

The Cedar Rapids area boasts more than 100 miles of bike trails to help you explore all sides of the city and connect you with surrounding towns. The Cedar Valley Nature Trail offers 51 miles of trails within Linn County alone, perfect for a day-long biking adventure. One of the most scenic trails in town is the Sac and Fox trail, a seven-mile, crushed limestone trail that wanders along Indian Creek and offers plenty of shade on sweltering summer days. If you are into mountain biking, there are several sites—including Beverly Park and Cheyenne Park BMX—that are designed for off trail adventures. What's great about the trail system in and around Cedar Rapids is that many of the trails connect, so you can design your own route depending on where you'd like to start or stop and what pit stops you'd like to make along the way.

linncountytrails.org

CYCLE AND SIP
AT CEDAR LAKE

Cedar Lake is soon going to be the most popular recreation spot in town. Currently a work in progress as the city embarks on reclaiming this outdoor recreation spot on the outskirts of downtown, Cedar Lake is a prime spot for biking enthusiasts. There is currently a paved trail that circles the lake, connecting to longer trails to the north and south. Water sports opportunities and a new boardwalk across the lake are much-anticipated features coming to the area. When you need a pit stop, hit up the Sag Wagon. This bar is a favorite not only for its picturesque location, but also because of the ample space to enjoy a cold beverage when you are biking your way through town. There are outdoor fire pits, sand volleyball courts, and splendid views of the sunset.

Sag Wagon
827 Shaver Rd. NE, 319-366-3265
thesagwagon.com

Cedar Lake
connectcr.org

TAKE A
TROPICAL ESCAPE
AT THE NOELRIDGE
GREENHOUSES AND GARDENS

A hidden gem in the heart of the city, the Noelridge Greenhouses are a tropical escape that is especially appealing during the frigid winter months. The greenhouses contain more than 600 varieties of plants from all around the world. You'll be greeted by banana trees and bromeliads and find the ground covered in ferns and mosses. There's a 50-year-old Bougainvillea tree, birds of paradise, a small pond, and even a desert space filled with succulents and cacti that reach to the ceiling. You'll be astounded as you take in more than 40 varieties of orchids as well.

4900 Council St. NE, 319-286-5762
cedar-rapids.org/residents/parks_and_recreation/noelridge_greenhouse.php

---

TIP

Pop back over to Noelridge Park in the summer to check out all the annuals planted in the gardens just outside the greenhouses. Maintained by the city's talented staff, the beds are a creative display of a wide variety of flowers artfully planted. It's a perfect spot for a picnic lunch.

• •

SNAG A TROUT
AT MCLOUD RUN STREAM

As the only urban trout stream in Iowa, this is a unique spot for avid anglers to check out. McLoud Run Stream is fed by a natural spring and runs for about two and a half miles—between Cedar Lake and 42nd Street Northeast—in a lightly wooded section of town right near the interstate. Anglers are likely to catch brown trout, rainbow trout, green sunfish, and white suckers, which the Department of Natural Resources stock regularly. There is a paved trail nearby—typically busy with bikers, runners, and walkers—and several picnic spots, as well as a small playground at one end of the stream. Do keep in mind that McLoud Run is a catch-and-release, artificial-lure-only regulation stream. So, snag as many trout as you can, but you must release them right back into the clear, cold water.

1819 McLoud Pl., 515-725-8200
iowadnr.gov/idnr/fishing/where-to-fish/trout-streams/stream-details/
lakecode/tmr57

TIP

If you work up an appetite fishing, stop in at
New Pioneer Food Co-op. This local, organic
grocery store offers a hot food bar, salad bar, deli
counter, and bakery with some of the best, most
nutritious foods you can find in town.

3338 Center Point Rd. NE, 319-365-2632
newpi.coop

SINK YOUR PUTT
AT TWIN PINES GOLF COURSE

If you are looking to pass the time on a summer afternoon, look no further than Twin Pines. Here you'll find Mini Pines, an 18-hole mini golf course that will have your whole family—young and old—entertained as you battle for family putting rights. Just swing clear of the nine-foot waterfall and pond at the center of the course. On the hottest of days, plan to go in the evening and play under the lights. Or if you feel like playing the long game, Twin Pines also has a full 18-hole golf course and a driving range. The fairways are generous, and it's one of the most popular courses in the state with junior and senior players alike. While the course is walkable, golf carts are available for rent.

3800 42nd St. NE, 319-286-5583
cedar-rapids.org/residents/parks_and_recreation/crgolf/
twin_pines_golf_course.php
cedar-rapids.org/residents/parks_and_recreation/crgolf/
mini_pines_miniature_golf_course.php

PLAY WITH NATURE
AT WICKIUP HILL
OUTDOOR LEARNING CENTER

Just north of Cedar Rapids in Toddville, this spot is particularly popular with families with young children. There is plenty of fun to be had indoors, exploring how Indigenous peoples lived off the land and how water impacts our rural and urban communities. There are several bird watching opportunities while you play in a treehouse or hide out in the bird blind. Outdoors you'll find the Wandering Woods, a natural playscape that encourages kids of all ages to find fun in the natural world around them. The zipline is always a hit with both the young and young at heart. Plus, Wickiup Hill offers miles of trails to wander—whether you are looking to promenade through the prairie, stroll along the boardwalk over the wetlands, or frolic through the forest.

10260 Morris Hill Rd., Toddville, 319-892-6485
linncountyiowa.gov/977/wickiup-hill-learning-center

FIND PEACE
AT PRAIRIEWOODS FRANCISCAN SPIRITUALITY CENTER

Perhaps the best place in the area to find a mindful, Zen-like experience is at Prairiewoods. On this 70-acre site, you can focus on ecology, spirituality, and holistic health. Visitors can wander the paths of the prairie to take in the tall grasses and imagine the land as it was decades before settlers started calling it home. Or you can stroll along the paths that weave and wander through the wooded portion of the property. This haven of peace, located in the heart of the city's northeast side, also offers a variety of spiritual, reflective, and creative workshops throughout the year along with holistic health services like massage and guided meditation. The on-site guest house, hermitages, and sweat lodge are options for those looking to extend their stay. The main building was also the first nonprofit in the state of Iowa to receive the US Green Building Council's LEED® Gold certification for an existing building, illustrating that Prairiewoods practices what it preaches as a steward of the environment.

120 Boyson Rd., Hiawatha, 319-395-6700
prairiewoods.org

PICK A BUSHEL OF APPLES
AT ALLEN'S ORCHARD

It's a known fact that homemade apple pie tastes that much sweeter if you plucked the apples from the trees yourself. If that thought alone makes your mouth water, head to Allen's Orchard on the north side of Marion. This family-owned orchard is over 50 years old and offers you-pick apples during the fall, typically from August through October. The orchard is full of 50 different varieties to pick from, too. Call or check Facebook before heading out to see which varieties are available for picking the day of your visit. There are also pears, concord grapes, and pumpkins available during the season as well. Before you leave Allen's, make sure to try an apple slushie and pick up a gallon of fresh apple cider, a pack of apple turnovers, and a pack of cherry donuts to enjoy at home. You can thank me later.

5801 N 10th St., Marion, 319-377-1408
allensorchard.com

CAMP OUT
AT PINICON RIDGE PARK

One of the best camping spots in the area, Pinicon Ridge Park offers 966 acres to explore along the Wapsipinicon River. Located just 15 miles north of Cedar Rapids, this county park is wooded and hilly and offers several hiking trails of different lengths for nature lovers to enjoy. Don't miss your chance to climb to the top of the Pinicon Ridge Observation Tower, where you'll enjoy the view more than 1,000 feet above sea level. You might also spot an American elk in the Alexander Wildlife Area at the south entrance to the park. The campground is open from mid-April through mid-October and is a favorite spot for family camping, whether in a tent, RV, or cabin. Equipment for a variety of water sports is available for rental as well.

4732 Horseshoe Falls Rd., Central City, 319-892-6450
mycountyparks.com/county/linn/park/pinicon-ridge-park.aspx

PICK OUT
A PERFECT PUMPKIN
AT LOCAL PUMPKIN PATCHES

There's something special about picking out the perfect pumpkin and plucking it right from the field. Luckily, several local spots make this experience possible each fall. For many, a visit to these pumpkin patches becomes a family tradition. These family-owned farms also turn a visit to the patch into a full celebration of the harvest season. You can not only buy cornstalks, gourds, and bundles of hay to transform your porch, but you can also enjoy a hayrack ride or an adventure through a corn maze. At Bart's Farm you can even go for a pony ride and visit some of the other farm animals. At Bass Farms, agri-tours are offered so you can learn more about all the crops grown on this sustainable farm. Their country store offers an incredible selection of baking mixes, sauces, fresh produce, and much more.

Bart's Farm and Pumpkin Patch
7307 Alburnett Rd., Marion, 319-373-2633
facebook.com/bartsfarmandpumpkinpatch

Bass Farms
840 Bass Ln., Mount Vernon, 319-895-6480
bassfarms.org

TAKE A WALK THROUGH THE WOODS
AT MORGAN CREEK PARK

A walk through the woods at Morgan Creek Park, just outside of Cedar Rapids near the town of Palo, is anything but ordinary, especially during the early spring when the woodland trail is carpeted with blooming bluebells. You'll also be amazed as you wander around the arboretum at Morgan Creek Park. It is filled with 250 species of trees—both native and exotic—many of which flower with spectacular, fragrant blossoms in the springtime. You'll be captivated by the variety of colors and scents. There are picnic pavilions constructed in the park—made from salvaged lumber from downed trees—making this a perfect spot to dine al fresco.

7517 Worcester Rd., Palo, 319-892-6450
mycountyparks.com/county/linn/park/morgan-creek-park.aspx

MAKE A SPLASH
AT CHERRY HILL POOL AND PARK

One of the city's most popular—and largest—municipal pools is the Cherry Hill Aquatic Center. Once you see the large slides, including a speed slide and a drop slide; the zero-depth entry; and the array of water features, including a lily pad ropes course and a large water playground, you'll understand why this is such a hit with families in the summer. Arrive early to snag a spot under one of the large shade umbrellas. Cherry Hill Park, which spans 46 acres, also offers several playgrounds to explore with the little ones. The paved trail that runs the circumference of the park is great for long walks and talks with friends, and features a story walk for families to read along with as they make the loop.

341 Stoney Point Rd. NW, 319-286-5792
cedar-rapids.org/residents/parks_and_recreation/cherry_hill_aquatic_center.php

---

TIP
Splash pads are located at various parks around the city, offering a no cost way to cool off on the hottest summer days.

GET ROWDY
AT A CEDAR RAPIDS
ROUGHRIDERS HOCKEY GAME

While hockey is not as much of a pastime in Iowa as it is in some surrounding states, Cedar Rapids is lucky enough to play host to the RoughRiders, a Tier 1 junior hockey team in the US Hockey League. Checking out a game is a must. But come prepared, as the atmosphere is rowdy and "the stable" gets loud with enthusiastic fans. Be sure to check the calendar to see what promotions and special events are taking place during any given home game. Feel free to bring your own cow bell to ring.

1100 Rockford Rd. SW, 319-247-0340
roughridershockey.com

TIP
When you are ready to lace up a pair of ice skates of your own, head over to the indoor public skating rink to take a few laps around the ice. You might also catch a demonstration by the Cedar Rapids Curling Club.

CHEER ON
THE BOYS OF SUMMER
AT THE CEDAR RAPIDS KERNELS

Play ball! Or rather, cheer on the boys of summer as they take to the baseball field at Veterans Memorial Stadium. Cedar Rapids is proud of its minor league baseball team, the Cedar Rapids Kernels, an affiliate of the Minnesota Twins. The atmosphere at the ballpark is always a ton of fun. Tickets are very reasonable, and the games are action packed. The concessions are mouthwatering—be sure to stop by the Mexican cart for delicious nachos and the shaved ice stand for a cool treat. And it's a party at the park for the kids, too. The family entertainment area with inflatables and games is always hopping. Games on Friday or Saturday nights are extra fun as they shoot off fireworks after the game. On Sundays, kids can run the bases after the game. Cheering on the Kernels is a win for the whole family.

950 Rockford Rd. SW, 319-896-7560
milb.com/cedar-rapids

REV YOUR ENGINE
AT HAWKEYE DOWNS

If you are looking for some fast, family fun, head to Hawkeye Downs. On Friday nights during the summer months, just follow the sounds of engines revving. You can catch several races whip around at breakneck speeds, including stock car racing, enduros, street drags, drifting expos, and more on the quarter-mile and half-mile banked asphalt tracks. While the site was home to a dirt racetrack beginning in the 1920s, the current raceway opened in 1989 as Iowa's first paved racetrack. It remains the only full-time weekly asphalt track in Iowa and has been a prime spot for speedy entertainment since. The property also features an expo hall where several special events happen throughout the year, including antique shows, craft shows, home and RV shows, and more.

4400 6th St. SW, 319-365-8656
hawkeyedowns.org

HIKE WITH A LLAMA
AT PRAIRIE PATCH FARM

It's not every day you get to lead a llama down a prairie path. But this private, 50-acre nature preserve and wildlife refuge just outside of town is a picturesque spot for just such a unique outdoor adventure. On your 90-minute llama hike, you'll take in the prairie, cross a creek or two, and wander through the forest, all while learning a bit more about the people-loving llamas accompanying you. Hikes are offered from April through December with a break in July and August to avoid the hottest months. If you aren't able to take a hike, check out options for selfies and snuggles, a llama-friendly picnic, or llama-gram visits to you or someone you love. All visits are by appointment only, so make sure to schedule your llama interactions in advance.

2991 120th St., 319-849-8066
prairiepatchfarm.com

HIKE THE BLUFFS
AT PALISADES-KEPLER STATE PARK

Located just a short drive to the east of Cedar Rapids, Palisades-Kepler State Park offers plenty of adventure. Whether you are looking to enjoy a picnic lunch on the banks of the river, or you are hoping to hike—a solid five miles—along the wooded bluffs, there are so many options to enjoy the great outdoors in this 840-acre park. There are rustic cabins available for rental at Palisades, as well as other overnight camping spots. The lodges and structures scattered throughout the park were built in the 1930s by the Civilian Conservation Corps. While the park is beautiful in any season, fall is a particularly picturesque time for a visit to take in the vivid colors of the trees that line the ravines and bluffs overlooking the Cedar River.

700 Kepler Dr., Mount Vernon, 319-895-6039
iowadnr.gov/places-to-go/state-parks/iowa-state-parks/
palisades-kepler-state-park

SAY BOO
AT BLOOMSBURY FARM

Bloomsbury Farm is a must-visit attraction during the month of October. This sprawling farm offers so many activities for the whole family, it's tough to pack it all in one day. One of the most notable features is the corn maze, with a fresh design each year for visitors to wander through. You can pick your own pumpkin in the 18-acre patch. There are goats, llamas, and other baby farm animals to feed. The little ones can explore the corn palace playground or take a barrel train ride. And there is a zipline for those looking for a quick thrill. Of course, for those brave enough to enter, there are several haunted houses to scream through once the sun goes down. The farm is being operated by fifth-generation farmers who delight in having turned their plot of Iowa farmland into an agri-tourism destination.

3260 69th St., Atkins, 319-446-7667
bloomsburyfarm.com

BRAVE THE WAVES
AT MANCHESTER WHITEWATER PARK

Manchester Whitewater Park is a fun day trip for those looking for some adventure on the water. Located just a 45-minute drive northeast of Cedar Rapids, this manufactured whitewater course features six 18-inch drops in the Maquoketa River and runs 800 feet along the length of downtown Manchester. A paved walking trail allows those wanting to ride the waves again and again to easily walk back to the start of the course. Tube rentals are available at several local businesses, but visitors are welcome to bring their own. Kayaks are also welcome. This free, adventure-filled experience is especially popular in the summer months. The park is technically open year-round. Public parking and restroom facilities are available as well. Life jackets are encouraged.

300 W Main St., Manchester, 563-927-3636
manchester-ia.org/whitewater-park

MAKE MOVIE DREAMS COME TRUE
AT FIELD OF DREAMS

No, this isn't heaven. It's Iowa, where you can find the *Field of Dreams* movie site in Dyersville, about a 45-minute drive to the northeast of Cedar Rapids. Made famous by the 1989 movie of the same name, starring Kevin Costner, the *Field of Dreams* movie site has been a popular tourist destination for decades. The movie was actually shot on-site, where they built the field next to a century old farmhouse—which you can also tour or now book an overnight stay in. Visitors to the site can run the bases, walk out into the corn, and grab a souvenir in the gift shop. In 2021, Major League Baseball erected a field next to the movie site and hosted an official MLB game between the New York Yankees and Chicago White Sox. Plans are in the works to have two MLB teams play in the farm-field setting each season. Batter up!

28995 Lansing Rd., Dyersville, 1-888-875-8404
fieldofdreamsmoviesite.com

CUT YOUR OWN BOUQUET
AT LOCAL FLOWER FARMS

Nothing brightens your day quicker than a bouquet of fresh flowers. Here you can take the experience up a notch by cutting and creating your very own bouquets. Typically open in July and August, several flower farms around the area offer visitors the opportunity to snip their own stems in their cutting gardens, which feature everything from dahlias and gladiolas to irises and hollyhocks. Whether you are looking to create bouquets to brighten up a room in your home or to make a special event like a baby shower or wedding celebration more festive, a visit to a flower farm is a unique summer joy.

Pheasant Run Farm
pheasantrunfarmiowa.com

Promise & Blossom
promiseandblossom.com/little-flower-farm

Lovely Bunches
lovelybunches.com

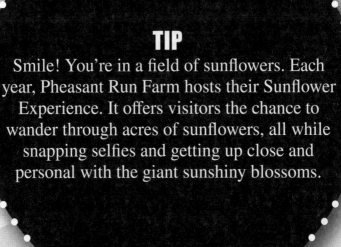

TIP

Smile! You're in a field of sunflowers. Each
year, Pheasant Run Farm hosts their Sunflower
Experience. It offers visitors the chance to
wander through acres of sunflowers, all while
snapping selfies and getting up close and
personal with the giant sunshiny blossoms.

THIS WINDOW
DEDICATED IN 1955
HONORS THE SACRED
MEMORY OF THE MEN
AND WOMEN WHO
UNSELFISHLY GAVE
THEIR LIVES IN DEFENSE
OF OUR COUNTRY.

Memorial Window, designed by Grant Wood, 1928-29.
Fabricated by Emil Frei Art Glass Company.
Photo courtesy of Veterans Memorial Commission and Fisheye Photography

CULTURE
AND HISTORY

IMMERSE YOURSELF IN ART
AT THE CEDAR RAPIDS MUSEUM OF ART

Known for its regional art collection, the Cedar Rapids Museum of Art is best known for its collection of works—the world's largest, in fact—by local protégé Grant Wood. Don't recognize the name? He's the famed creator of *American Gothic*. While you won't see that iconic painting hanging in Cedar Rapids—it lives at the Art Institute of Chicago—you will see a whole host of works by Wood and other acclaimed regional artists along with a continually changing special exhibition schedule displaying a variety of art media spanning centuries. The Museum also boasts an eclectic shop where you can snag an art-themed gift or your own piece of artwork created by a local artist to start or add to your own private collection. A stunning atrium filled with a surprising selection of tropical flora greets you when you first set foot inside.

410 3rd St. SE, 319-366-7503
crma.org

STEP INTO
AN ARTIST'S HOME
AT THE GRANT WOOD STUDIO

After you check out Grant Wood's many masterpieces at the Cedar Rapids Museum of Art, head a few blocks east, where you can enter the very studio where Wood painted *American Gothic* and so many of his famed works. The artist lived and worked in this small studio apartment in the carriage house owned by a prominent family that included some of Wood's many local benefactors. For a time, he even shared the small space with his mother and sister. A tour guide will share unique stories of Wood's days living and working in Cedar Rapids during your visit, including how he had his studio set up and the parties he hosted. Pay close attention as you enter the studio, as you'll spot some of Wood's humor and charm in the custom front door he crafted.

810 2nd Ave. SE, 319-366-7503
crma.org/grant-wood/grant-wood-studio

LOOK INTO
LOCAL HISTORY
AT THE HISTORY CENTER

Home of the Linn County Historical Society, The History Center is a museum that offers a glimpse into what makes Cedar Rapids and the surrounding area—all of Linn County—unique. Even the museum's location—in the historic Douglas Mansion—is a beautiful, fitting location for its mission to help connect visitors of all ages to the past and its influence on the present and future. The museum has permanent and changing exhibitions to display some of the 50,000 items in their collection donated by individuals and local businesses. Be sure to not only take in the beauty of the mansion—especially the grand staircase—but also learn about the home's rich history, as it has served as a family home, a funeral home, and more.

800 2nd Ave., 319-362-1501
historycenter.org

READ A BOOK ON THE ROOF
AT THE CEDAR RAPIDS PUBLIC LIBRARY

Popping into the downtown branch of the Cedar Rapids Public Library isn't just about grabbing a book to read. The library was rebuilt in 2013 after a devastating flood ravaged the former downtown main branch of the Cedar Rapids Public Library in 2008. The new building boasts a modern design that is both whimsical and inviting for residents and visitors alike. The youngest readers can crawl through a tunnel to enter the children's section and will have fun exploring all this area has to offer, including interesting spots to curl up with a book. Then grab a coffee from the local coffee shop located in the lobby. Don't miss out on heading up to the living roof, where you can take in the fresh air and see native plants thriving several stories up in the center of the downtown hub. Relax and read a book while soaking up the sun.

450 5th Ave. SE, 319-291-READ
crlibrary.org

HONOR THOSE WHO SERVED OUR COUNTRY
AT VETERANS MEMORIAL BUILDING

On Mays Island in the heart of Cedar Rapids, you'll find the Veterans Memorial Building. Inside are three main spaces that now serve as stunning rental opportunities—a grand, expansive coliseum, an armory space in the basement, and a fourth-floor ballroom overlooking the river—for weddings, large meetings, community events, and even roller derby matches. But don't miss the museum galleries off the main lobby on the first floor, where you can see a variety of military memorabilia detailing the service rendered to our country over the years by local soldiers. The whole facility is managed by the Veterans Memorial Commission of the City of Cedar Rapids. It's a stunning architectural feature that sets the Cedar Rapids skyline apart and pays tribute to the contributions of veterans.

50 2nd Ave. Bridge, 319-286-5038
cedar-rapids.org/veteransmemorial

TIP

Not to be missed on your visit to the building is the exquisite Grant Wood Memorial Window. Best viewed as sunlight streams into the lobby, this 1928 stained glass masterpiece—20 feet wide by 24 feet tall—was created by famed artist Grant Wood to pay sparkling tribute to veterans. At the time of its installation, it was thought to be the largest stained glass window in the country.

PEEP PUBLIC ART
AROUND CEDAR RAPIDS

All around the Cedar Rapids area are a variety of sculptures, fountains, statues, and murals to discover. A recent reinvestment in and awareness of the importance of public art projects has helped some long-standing city art pieces—including such works as *Heart of the Matter* in Poet's Park—to be joined by other large sculptures that mark the entrance to a neighborhood, city event space, or park—such as *Regeneration*, which sits outside the Cedar Rapids Public Library. The large, colorful ceramic heads by artist Jun Kaneko outside the Cedar Rapids Museum of Art also offer a fun selfie opportunity. A variety of murals have cropped up, due in part to the efforts of a nonprofit organization called Murals and More, that offer pops of color, especially in the downtown core and the NewBo/Czech Village neighborhoods. Whether pulling inspiration from graffiti artists or historic Czech and Slovak images, the murals bring new life to buildings, skywalks, and parking ramps.

cedar-rapids.org/local_government/city_boards_and_commissions/
visual_arts_commission.php

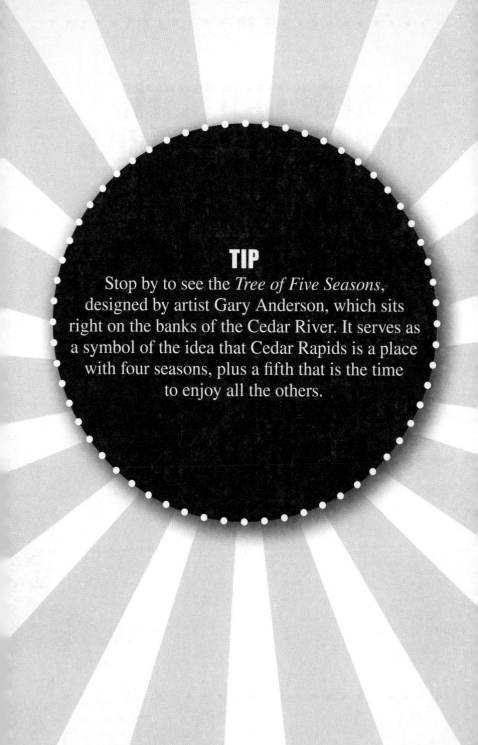

TIP

Stop by to see the *Tree of Five Seasons*, designed by artist Gary Anderson, which sits right on the banks of the Cedar River. It serves as a symbol of the idea that Cedar Rapids is a place with four seasons, plus a fifth that is the time to enjoy all the others.

STOP AND SMELL THE CRUNCHBERRIES
AT QUAKER OATS

Quaker Oats is the world's largest cereal factory and has been operating in Cedar Rapids since the late 1800s. While many are disappointed to find out that the company does not offer tours of the factory—adding some Willy Wonka's Chocolate Factory intrigue—it's hard to miss the expansive building with its iconic vintage neon sign on top as you drive through town. A uniquely Cedar Rapids experience you might have is that on certain days of the week, all of downtown will smell like sugary-sweet Captain Crunch Crunchberries. So, while you may not be able to see how they make the many other popular Quaker Oats products while you are in town, you can stop and smell the crunchberries.

418 2nd St. NE, 319-368-9840
quakeroats.com

GET IN TOUCH WITH THE HISTORY OF BLACK IOWANS
AT THE AFRICAN AMERICAN MUSEUM OF IOWA

The African American Museum of Iowa serves as the only statewide museum dedicated to preserving and telling the story of the African American experience in Cedar Rapids, the state of Iowa, and the nation as a whole. And the Museum takes its role very seriously. There are regular and traveling exhibitions to explore, each designed to help visitors trace Iowa's African American history from past to present. The permanent "Endless Possibilities" exhibit examines the desegregation of Iowa's public schools in 1868 and the fact that Iowans were holding sit-ins long before the Civil Rights Movement took off in other parts of the country. The museum also hosts a number of educational programs and special events throughout the year and has a small gift shop to peruse.

55 12th Ave. SE, 319-862-2101
blackiowa.org

CHECK OUT CZECH AND SLOVAK HISTORY
AT THE NATIONAL CZECH & SLOVAK MUSEUM & LIBRARY

Years ago, many immigrants from then Czechia found a home in Cedar Rapids upon coming to America. So, it's no surprise that Cedar Rapids is now home to the National Czech & Slovak Museum & Library. A premiere institution for collecting, preserving, and interpreting the history and culture of the Czech Republic and Slovakia, the museum displays its collection in permanent and changing exhibitions. You can tour an immigrant home, experience what it might have been like to travel on a steamship to America, or imagine living through World War II. The museum hosts traveling exhibitions from around the world throughout the year to add additional interactive learning opportunities, both historically framed and connected to the modern-day Czech and Slovak experiences. Be sure to tap into the variety of heritage programming, such as needlepoint lessons and folk egg-decorating. The museum store is a treasure trove of unique gifts and memorabilia, most notably stunning jewelry and hand-painted glass ornaments.

FUN FACT

The 2008 Flood in Cedar Rapids caused
some $9 million in damage to the museum.
To help better prepare the museum for future
flooding, the entire building, weighing in at
1,500 tons, was moved some 480 feet across
the street to higher ground. It reopened in its
current, higher location in 2012.

1400 Inspiration Pl. SW, 319-362-8500
ncsml.org

BRING HISTORY TO LIFE
AT BRUCEMORE

Built in 1886, Brucemore was home to prominent Cedar
Rapidians for three generations. Today the estate is part of the
National Trust for Historic Preservation, the only such site in
Iowa. Self-guided and guided tours are available of the stately
Queen Anne–style, three-story home, where visitors can learn
more about the immigrants, philanthropists, industrialists, and
children that built their lives here. The home is situated in the
middle of a 26-acre, parklike property in the heart of Cedar
Rapids. After touring the home, make sure to walk around
the grounds to see the gardens—a spectacular maze of color
and beauty, especially in summer months—the turtles sunning
themselves near the pond, and the large front lawn that serves
as the site of community events throughout the year. Other
special events throughout the year include theater productions
on a specially constructed outdoor stage, an arts festival, and
musical performances.

TIP

Brucemore gets dolled up for the holidays, so the Christmas season is a wonderful time to explore the mansion and its many rooms.

2160 Linden Dr. SE, 319-362-7375
brucemore.org

GRAB A SARSAPARILLA SODA
AT USHER'S FERRY HISTORIC VILLAGE

In a picturesque corner of Cedar Rapids's northeast side, you can step into a small Iowa town at the turn of the 20th century. Usher's Ferry Historic Village is a 10-acre site located near Seminole Valley Park. It features some 20 historic buildings that help visitors envision what life was like in the area more than a century ago, between 1890 and 1910. There is a gazebo at the heart of the village, a schoolhouse, and a traditional home among other buildings. Nine of the buildings are handicapped-accessible and open for tours. A highlight is grabbing a sarsaparilla soda in the saloon. Pay attention to the event schedule for the year to catch special activities like hayrack rides and adventure camps for kids. The city also recently added a lodge to the site for hosting a variety of events, from wedding receptions to business meetings.

TIP

Take a hike along the river and through Seminole Valley Park while in the area. This hidden gem of a city park has lots of wide-open spaces for flying kites, enjoying a picnic, or cross-country skiing in the winter. There's also a cricket pitch where matches between local cricket clubs take place each weekend throughout the summer.

5925 Seminole Valley Trail NE, 319-286-5763
cedar-rapids.org/residents/parks_and_
recreation/ushers_ferry_historic_
village.php

INVEST IN ART
AT THE MARION ARTS FESTIVAL

On the third Saturday of May each year since 1992, Marion Square Park in Cedar Rapids's neighboring city Marion has been taken over by art. Tents pop up along the walkways so that local, regional, and national artists can sell their works to patrons of the arts. The artists, selected by a jury each year, work in nearly every medium from pastels, photography, drawings, and fiber arts to jewelry, ceramics, glass, and metalwork, so there truly is art for everyone to appreciate. The event also includes a public art project that benefits local food pantries. Local musical entertainment and food vendors give the day a true festival feel.

City Square Park, Marion
marionartsfestival.com

TIP

Wander over to see the Uptown Marion Artway. This reimagined gathering space, once a drab and under-utilized alley, is now a hub of activity and a great spot to enjoy a treat or a chat with friends while enjoying nine permanent art installations by local and national artists.

uptownmarion.com/discover-uptown/ uptown-artway

VISIT A FRANK LLOYD WRIGHT HOME
AT CEDAR ROCK STATE PARK

The Walter Estate at Cedar Rock is truly a hidden gem for enthusiasts of interior design and the acclaimed architect Frank Lloyd Wright. An example of his Usoian residential style, the home was designed for Lowell and Agnes Walter in their retirement and is tucked away on a lovely parcel of land just outside of Quasqueton. Nearly every detail of the home—including furniture, carpets, and draperies that he picked out—bears the signature style of the famed architect, so Cedar Rock is considered one of Frank Lloyd Wright's most complete designs. The architect visited the Walters in their home shortly after its completion in 1950. If you'd like to see the interior of the home, you should visit between late May and early October and make reservations in advance.

2611 Quasqueton Diagonal Blvd., Independence, 319-934-3572
friendsofcedarrock.org

LEARN ABOUT
THE 31ST PRESIDENT
AT THE HERBERT HOOVER
PRESIDENTIAL LIBRARY AND MUSEUM

While not located in Cedar Rapids, the Herbert Hoover Presidential Library and Museum is just a 30-minute drive southeast and worth a visit. As Iowa's only presidential library and museum—and one of only 14 such institutions across the country thus far—it's a fantastic spot to learn more about President Hoover and his life. He only spent a decade living in Iowa as a child, fishing and helping on the farm, before he was orphaned and moved out of state to live with other family members. During a visit to the galleries, you'll also learn more about Hoover's family, including his wife Lou Henry Hoover, and some of his accomplishments and contributions to this country and history, including Hoover ball and the Hoover Dam. You'll come away from the visit realizing the pride that Iowans have in their connection to the 31st President of the United States.

210 Parkside Dr., West Branch, 319-643-5301
hoover.archives.gov

EAT AND SHOP YOUR WAY THROUGH
THE AMANA COLONIES

Willkommen to the Amana Colonies. Just a 30-minute drive south of Cedar Rapids, the Amana Colonies offer an opportunity to step into authentic German heritage in the heart of Eastern Iowa. What served as a communal living environment for German immigrants for more than 90 years is now not only a residential community but also a popular tourist destination and a National Historic Landmark. There are seven different villages to visit, each offering quaint shops, distinctive restaurants and breweries, and museums where you can learn more about how the people who called this area home lived, worked, and played together for decades. The area plays host to several festivals each year, including Winterfest, Maifest, Oktoberfest, and the Prelude to Christmas with the Tannenbaum Forest, which draw in large crowds and offer extra fun to visitors. No matter the time of year you visit, it's easy to spend a day or two wandering the Amana Colonies.

TIP

Plan a stay at Hotel Millwright while in the Amana Colonies. Once the site of the community's large woolen mill operation and the hub of the villages, it is now home to a 65-room boutique hotel after the textile factory was renovated into a space with touches of history and modern comforts. You can also take home as a souvenir an exquisite woolen blanket created at the still-functioning Amana Woolen Mill.

Hotel Millwright
800 48th Ave., Amana, 319-838-5015
hotelmillwright.com

Amana Colonies Convention and Visitors Bureau
622 46th Ave., Amana, 319-622-7622
amanacolonies.com

HOSE CO. NO. 4

1111

scribe
STATIONER

SHOPPING
AND FASHION

FIND THE PERFECT GIFT
AT SCOUT OF MARION

One peek at the vintage tile floor when you step inside of
SCOUT of Marion, and you'll fall in love with this beautiful
boutique. The shop's team scours the country to find products
from companies that care, bringing together an incredible
selection of home goods, personal care items, pantry essentials,
and gifts for kids, adults, your pets, and yourself. Each display
shelf and tablescape offers a curated selection of goods you'll
want to take home or that will make the perfect gift. You can
also sample and purchase artisan cheeses at the cheese counter.
It's an immersive shopping experience, with beautiful things to
see, smell, taste, and feel.

725 11th St., Marion, 319-373-1099
scoutofmarion.com

TIP

While in Marion, pop over to the West End shopping district, where you'll find cute little retail pop-up shops. Grab a book at Swamp Fox Bookstore. Find a new home accessory at Staged Dwellings or Juniper Company. Snag cute baby accessories at The Purple Wagon. And don't forget to get a bite to eat at the West End Diner.

West End Shops and Diner
809 6th Ave., Marion, 319-892-3012
westendmarion.com

INVIGORATE YOUR WARDROBE
AT LOCAL WOMEN'S BOUTIQUES

When you need a day out for a shopping spree, check out several local female-owned women's clothing boutiques. These shops have a wide selection of brands you won't find in other stores around town, and they can have you putting your best fashion foot forward whether you are headed out for a night on the town, spending a day in the office, or just lounging around at home. Each boutique has a style all its own, pulled together by the savvy shop owners. At JOY you are sure to find a unique piece or hidden gem. Don't forget to peek inside the former bank vault. At MODE, you'll find something stylish for every season, great denim, and even some giftable items. And at LA Trends Addict & Lynn's Boutique, you'll find trendy, new arrivals every week in a range of sizes (XS-3XL).

JOY
710 11th St., Marion, 319-377-0866
joyinmarion.com

MODE
1394 Twixt Town Rd., Marion, 319-826-6552
modeiowa.com

LA Trends Addict & Lynn's Boutique
1200 N Center Point Rd., Hiawatha, 319-200-2222
latrendsaddict.com

TOAST THE TOWN
AT 1ST AVENUE WINE HOUSE

1st Avenue Wine House is stocked with boutique wines, both domestic and international, so it's great whether you are looking to grab a bottle of wine for dinner or hosting a gathering with friends. Best of all, the owner is incredibly knowledgeable about wine and helps every customer select something that is right for their palate and their pocketbook. The store's unique setting in a large, old home invites visitors to wander from room to room checking out a variety of wines, snacks, accessories, and giftable items. If you are looking for a quick thank-you or celebratory offering, snag one of the festive gift baskets that the store always has made up and ready to go. The lovely courtyard outside serves as the perfect setting for tastings and live music. There's always a sweet shop dog to greet you as well.

3412 1st Ave. NE, 319-298-9463
1stavenuewinehouse.com

PICK UP A PLANT
AT LOCAL NURSERIES

If you are a plant lover, there's a whole host of shops to visit around town, each with its distinctive style. Head to Moss Plant Shop for a clean, modern approach to plant care and to see the incredible moss art installation on the wall. At Blooms, don't miss the build-your-fairy-garden bar tucked in among the houseplants. Roots & Bloom offers a romantic and whimsical approach to floral arrangements. And Pierson's Floral Shop and Greenhouse has the most incredible selection of orchids in town.

Moss Plant Shop
74 16th Ave. SW, 319-200-1082
mossplantshop.com

Cedar River Garden Center
2889 Palo Marsh Rd., Palo
319-851-2161
cedarrivergardencenter.com

Blooms Garden Center & Gift Shop
1440 Blairs Ferry Rd. NE
319-329-7178
bloomsgardencenter.com

Pierson's Floral
1800 Ellis Blvd. NW, 319-366-1826
piersonsflowershop.com

Roots in Bloom
524 10th St., Marion, 319-377-9312
rootsinbloom.org

SEE AND BE SEEN
AT THE DOWNTOWN FARMERS MARKET

The highlight of summer in downtown Cedar Rapids is Saturday mornings spent at the farmers market. For nearly 20 years, the market has popped up from 8 a.m. to noon on eight Saturdays between the end of May to mid-September. It has grown to become one of the largest open-air markets in the Midwest. The Cedar Rapids Downtown Farmers Market spans several city blocks and features vendors selling fresh produce, meats, cheeses, wine, artisan crafts, jewelry, and more. Plus, there's a regular line up of entertainers, from local dance groups to *American Idol* contestants, to keep the market environment festive. Bring your own bag and come prepared to leave the market with a full belly and an armload of fresh foods and unique finds. Check the website to find out dates for the market and the year's official market map.

cedarrapids.org/events/farmers-market

TIP

On Saturdays when Cedar Rapids is not hosting its market, head over to Marion Square Park to enjoy the Uptown Market. It's a smaller-scale market, but it still offers plenty of fresh produce, tasty treats, and entertainment for the whole family.
marioncc.org/uptown-marion-markets.html

ADD TO YOUR ART COLLECTION
AT GILDED PEAR GALLERY

Cedar Rapids is a creative community, and one of the best spots to witness this firsthand is Gilded Pear Gallery. In a bright, two-story gallery space on the edge of downtown, this woman-owned contemporary gallery curates an impressive collection of works by more than 70 artists from around the Midwest and the country. There are sweeping landscape paintings. There are vibrant, modern pieces with large swathes of color. There are sculptures, fiber arts, ceramics, photography, works in glass, and even jewelry that are true signature pieces and conversation starters. A wide variety of price points are available as well, making the gallery accessible to seasoned art collectors or those just starting a personal collection. Special exhibitions, of both individual artists and group shows, are changed out every six to eight weeks throughout the year. And the expert art handlers at Gilded Pear also offer framing.

808 3rd Ave. SE, 319-366-0205
gildedpeargallery.com

SNAG A SNARKY TEE
AT RAYGUN

Welcome to the greatest store in the universe, or so they say. The store—one of several locations across the Midwest—is known for its whip-smart sayings and its quick turnaround time for printing timely messages on t-shirts. Cedar Rapids sayings include "See the Rabbits" and "We built this city on cereal." You'll also find sayings that refer to other cities, the Midwest in general, sports teams, and current events and politics. More than just words on shirts, RAYGUN also sells, glasses, posters, keychains, magnets, postcards, stickers, and more. RAYGUN is a union shop and store, and all products are created in Des Moines, Iowa. A portion of all sales goes to charity causes as well. You are sure to find a snarky comment that hits home for you or someone you know as you wander around the store.

1028 3rd St. SE, 319-200-4083
raygunsite.com/collections/cedar-rapids

MEET AN ARTIST
AT IOWA CERAMICS CENTER
AND GLASS STUDIO

The Iowa Ceramics Center and Glass Studio is a hub of creative activity. On any given day that you stop by you are likely to see an artist at work in the space. In fact, the studio hosts visiting artists each year who work to hone their craft and are always happy to chat with visitors. A variety of classes in clay and warm glass—from ceramic wheel throwing and coil-pot workshops to glass ornament and vase classes—are offered for all ages and skill levels as well. An eclectic gallery space is filled with the work of resident artists and has an offering of original clay and glass work available for purchase.

Iowa Ceramics Center and Glass Studio
329 10th Ave. SE, Ste. 117, 319-365-9644
iowaceramicscenter.org

TIP

The historic Cherry Building where the Ceramics Center makes its home is a longtime fixture of the NewBo neighborhood. Once serving as a factory where dairy equipment was made, the building is now home to artist studios—check out the work of Akwi Nji, Kathy Schumacher, and John Schwartzkopf—as well as other creative small businesses and shops including Illuminations Center for Enlightenment and Mad Modern vintage furniture. Don't miss the opportunity to snap a picture with the cherry sculpture outside the rear entrance to the building.

The Cherry Building
329 10th Ave. SE, Cedar Rapids, 319-366-7026
facebook.com/thecherrybuilding

PICK UP
YOUR NEXT READ
AT NEXT PAGE BOOKS

If your city doesn't have an independent bookstore, is it even really a city? Cedar Rapids is lucky enough to have Next Page Books. Here you can find floor-to-ceiling bookshelves stacked with fiction, nonfiction, young adult, and children's titles, something for every literary interest. If they don't have what you are looking for in stock, the store owner is quick to place a special order to get your next great read in your hands. Be sure to say hello to shop cat Frank while you are shopping. Next Page Books also plays host to a book club and various events with local, regional, and national authors throughout the year where you can meet with your favorites and have a book signed.

1105 3rd St. SE, 319-247-2665
npbnewbo.com

TIP

If music is more your thing, pop around the corner and check out Analog Vault, a local record shop where they buy and sell vinyl records and turntables and offer repairs on vintage hi-fi pieces.
215 11th Ave. SE, 319-558-6853, analogvaultcr.com

WRITE YOUR PEN PAL
AT SCRIBE STATIONER

This new kid on the block in the NewBo area is tucked into the first floor of the neighborhood's original firehouse, which was built in 1916. Ogle the incredible white and green subway tile and make sure you look for the spot where the brass fire pole was once located. This dreamy shop is dedicated to the art of letter-writing. Full of journals, note cards and stationery, fountain pens, calligraphy supplies, and the like, this is a must-stop shop for anyone who appreciates finding a letter from a friend in their mailbox. In an effort to keep the art of old-style letter-writing alive and well, there's even a vintage typewriter where you can tap out a letter to a friend that the shop will mail for you. This charming brick building is a favorite spot for local photographers to stop and snap family and senior pictures as well.

1111 3rd St. SE, 319-200-1762, scribeiowa.com

TIP
Hose House No. 4 also now hosts a unique Airbnb on the second floor of the former firehouse that gives a nod to the building's past life. Check in for the weekend or the week, and you'll not only enjoy the cozy, firefighter-themed accommodations but also be right in the heart of all the fun just right outside the front door.

SHOP SMALL
IN THE CZECH VILLAGE

The Czech Village is a historic and distinctive neighborhood on the banks of the Cedar River, just south of downtown and across the Bridge of Lions. Here you can find a wide variety of local boutiques to delight shoppers young and old. There are vintage finds, imports from Slovakia and the Czech Republic, hand-crafted treasures, stylish closet staples, home accessories, sweet treats, and more. Shoppers can find something for themselves, for their home, or for a gift. You'll be pleasantly surprised by the shopping opportunities as you make your way down both sides of 16th Avenue. What was once a hub of activity for the Czech and Slovak immigrants making Cedar Rapids their new home, is now a community gathering place and a daytime destination for shopping, food, and fun.

Found and Formed
65 16th Ave. SW, 319-438-2727
foundandformedshop.com

Frolics Village Boutique
72 16th Ave. SW, 319-486-0924
frolicsboutique.com

Vintage Market and Supply Co.
95 16th Ave. SW, 319-200-4555
facebook.com/vintagemarket.village

Sweet Mercantile Soda Fountain & Candy Shop
98 16th Ave. SW, 319-200-7766
sweetmercantilecr.com

The Czech Cottage
100 16th Ave. SW, 319-366-4937
czechcottage.com

DOBRY Gift + Home
101 16th Ave. SW, 319-449-4081
dobryhome.com

Funky Zebras
102 16th Ave. SW, 319-361-9668
thefunkyzebras.com/locations/cedar-rapids-store

Garden Wren Florist & Yarn
102 16th Ave. SW, 319-241-9987
thegardenwren.com

CLIMB A ROCK WALL
AT SOKO OUTFITTERS

Not many stores have an indoor climbing wall, but at SOKO Outfitters in the Czech Village this adventurous feature is a perfect fit. Visitors to the premier destination for outdoor gear in the Cedar Rapids area can get outfitted for their next hike or get in a quick practice climb up the wall. Shoppers can find men's and women's clothing—featuring brands like Patagonia, Cotopaxi, and Fjallraven—as well as backpacks, hiking and camping supplies, outdoor furniture, and more. During the winter you can rent snowshoes and snow trekkers. During warmer weather, you can also rent kayaks and stand-up paddleboards, which are perfect for taking out on several local waterways. Once you are ready to purchase your own, the adventure-loving team at SOKO can help get you the right fit.

41 16th Ave. SW, 319-200-4848
sokooutfitters.com

EXPERIENCE SMALL TOWN HOSPITALITY
IN MOUNT VERNON

Mount Vernon is just a 15-minute drive from the southeast side of Cedar Rapids. Here you'll find oodles of small-town charm as you shop the three blocks of the uptown district. The city is well known for its art galleries and antique shops—Alice's Wonderland, Polly Ann's Vintage Market, The Shops at First Brick, and Mount Vernon Creates are a few favorites—as well as other boutiques, such as Silver Spider, Scarlet Boutique, Iron Leaf Press, and Bauman's, where you can find necessities and luxuries alike. In the old schoolhouse you'll find even more shops, including Blooming Acres and Helios Stitches N Stuff. There are also a few delectable spots to stop for a drink, treat, or meal. Don't miss Fuel, Palisades Café, Glyn Mawr Winery-The Local, and The Lincoln Wine Bar. Mount Vernon also plays host to a variety of special events throughout the year, so consider visiting during the Lincoln Highway Antique Fair on the 4th of July or during Magical Night to kick off the holiday shopping season. Chalk the Walk is a crowd favorite festival at the beginning of May, where artisans take over Main Street with vibrant chalk drawings.

visitmvl.com/shopping

ACTIVITIES
BY SEASON

Remember, Cedar Rapids is the City of Five Seasons . . . spring, summer, fall, and winter, plus a fifth season to enjoy them all. While many of the things listed in this book can be enjoyed any time of year, paying attention to the weather and the calendar can help you prioritize your fun.

SPRING

Order Up Some Seafood at Boston's, 22
Bike Around Town on Cedar Valley Trails, 69
Pick Up a Plant at Local Nurseries, 122
Invest in Art at the Marion Arts Festival, 110
Play with Nature at Wickiup Hill Outdoor Learning Center, 75
Explore Outer Space at Eastern Iowa Observatory, 60
Watch the Birds at Indian Creek Nature Center, 64
Take a Walk through the Woods at Morgan Creek Park, 80
Invigorate Your Wardrobe at Local Women's Boutiques, 120
Read a Book on the Roof at the Cedar Rapids Public Library, 97

SUMMER

Hear Symphony Music under the Stars at Brucemorchestra, 48

Snag a Scoop at Dan and Debbie's Creamery, 12

Celebrate Independence at the Cedar Rapids Freedom Festival, 56

See a Ski Show on the Cedar River, 54

Sink Your Putt at Twin Pines Golf Course, 74

See and Be Seen at the Downtown Farmers Market, 123

Cut Your Own Bouquet at Local Flower Farms, 90

Camp Out at Pinicon Ridge Park, 78

Savor Wood-Fired Pizza at a Local Farm, 24

Grab a Hot Dog at The Flying Wienie, 11

Brave the Waves at Manchester Whitewater Park, 88

Cheer On the Boys of Summer at the Cedar Rapids Kernels, 83

FALL

Enjoy Cider and Sliders at Sutliff Farm and Cider House, 4

Spend a Day on the Farm at Wilson's Orchard, 61

Pick a Bushel of Apples at Allen's Orchard, 77

Say Boo at Bloomsbury Farm, 87

Pick Out a Perfect Pumpkin at Local Pumpkin Patches, 79

Hike with a Llama at Prairie Patch Farm, 85

Grab a Sarsaparilla Soda at Usher's Ferry Historic Village, 108

Hike the Bluffs at Palisades-Kepler State Park, 86

Grab a Brew at Lion Bridge Brewing Company, 6

Snag a Trout at McLoud Run Stream, 72

Dine Al Fresco at General Store Pub, 43

• •

WINTER

Take a Tropical Escape at the Noelridge Greenhouses and Gardens, 71

Climb a Rock Wall at SOKO Outfitters, 132

Immerse Yourself in Art at the Cedar Rapids Museum of Art, 94

Gather with Friends at LP Street Food, 31

Pick Up Your Next Read at Next Page Books, 128

Find the Perfect Gift at SCOUT of Marion, 118

Shop Small in the Czech Village, 130

Get Rowdy at a Cedar Rapids Roughriders Hockey Game, 82

Have a Fancy Feast at Cobble Hill, 2

Cozy Up at Giving Tree Theater, 58

Get in Touch with the History of Black Iowans
    at the African American Museum of Iowa, 103

• •

SUGGESTED
ITINERARIES

DAY TRIPS FROM CR

Eat on Main Street in Solon, 44

Experience Small Town Hospitality in Mount Vernon, 133

Eat and Shop Your Way through the Amana Colonies, 114

Dine Al Fresco at General Store Pub, 43

Spend a Day on the Farm at Wilson's Orchard, 61

Camp Out at Pinicon Ridge Park, 78

Make Movie Dreams Come True at Field of Dreams, 89

KEEP THE KIDS BUSY

Start Your Day with a Sweet Treat at Donutland, 13

Snag a Scoop at Dan and Debbie's Creamery, 12

Explore Outer Space at Eastern Iowa Observatory, 60

Sink Your Putt at Twin Pines Golf Course, 74

Play with Nature at Wickiup Hill Outdoor Learning Center, 75

Say Boo at Bloomsbury Farm, 87

Make a Splash at Cherry Hill Pool and Park, 81

Sling a Slice at Local Pizza Joints, 14

Celebrate Independence at the Cedar Rapids Freedom Festival, 56

Pet Baby Animals at Old MacDonald's Farm, 66

Grab a Sarsaparilla Soda at Usher's Ferry Historic Village, 108

· ·

GIRLS' WEEKEND

Sample Iowa Wine and Spirits at Cedar Ridge Winery and Distillery, 5

Invigorate Your Wardrobe at Local Women's Boutiques, 120

Toast the Town at 1st Avenue Wine House, 121

Write Your Pen Pal at Scribe Stationer, 129

Shop Small in the Czech Village, 130

Fill Your Mug at Local Coffee Shops, 36

Find the Perfect Gift at SCOUT of Marion, 118

Bring History to Life at Brucemore, 106

Cut Your Own Bouquet at Local Flower Farms, 90

Feast on Inventive Pizza at Fong's, 10

FOR HISTORY BUFFS

Look into Local History at the History Center, 96

Travel Back in Time at Lighthouse Inn Supper Club, 42

Toast a Bit of History at Little Bohemia, 29

Peek at Memorabilia at Irish Democrat, 16

Learn about the 31st President at the Herbert Hoover Presidential Library and Museum, 113

Step into an Artist's Home at the Grant Wood Studio, 95

Eat Kolaches at Sykora Bakery, 8

Honor Those Who Served Our Country at Veterans Memorial Building, 98

• •

FOODIE FAVORITES

Tantalize Your Tastebuds at NewBo City Market, 3

Have a Fancy Feast at Cobble Hill, 2

Eat Your Way through Marion, 38

Grab a Brew at Lion Bridge Brewing Company, 6

Celebrate Taco Tuesday at Caucho, 9

Buy Your Bread at Rustic Hearth Bakery, 41

Give Back While Eating 'Cue at Willie Ray's Q Shack, 21

Dine Among the Stacks at R.G. Books and Vino's Ristorante, 20

Pick a Bushel of Apples at Allen's Orchard, 77

Enjoy a Class Act Meal at the Hotel at Kirkwood Center, 28

Fill Your Belly at Made-from-Scratch Cafés, 32

Jive to Some Jazz at Jazz Under the Stars, 57

OFF THE BEATEN PATH

Savor Wood-Fired Pizza at a Local Farm, 24

Hear World Music at CSPS, 49

Visit a Frank Lloyd Wright Home at Cedar Rock State Park, 112

Snag a Trout at McLoud Run Stream, 72

Share a Sweet Treat at Kava House & Café, 40

Hike with a Llama at Prairie Patch Farm, 85

Grab a Hot Dog at The Flying Wienie, 11

Brave the Waves at Manchester Whitewater Park, 88

Take a Walk through the Woods at Morgan Creek Park, 80

• •

OUTDOOR ADVENTURES

Find Peace at Prairiewoods Franciscan Spirituality Center, 76

Play, Practice, and Party at Lowe Park, 59

Hike the Bluffs at Palisades-Kepler State Park, 86

See and Be Seen at the Downtown Farmers Market, 123

Catch a Concert at McGrath Amphitheatre, 50

Watch the Birds at Indian Creek Nature Center, 64

Catch a Fish at Prairie Park Fishery, 68

Conquer the Climb at Mount Trashmore Trails & Overlook, 67

Pick Out a Perfect Pumpkin at Local Pumpkin Patches, 79

• •

INDEX

1st Avenue Wine House, 121

350 First, 30

African American Museum of Iowa, 103

Allen's Orchard, 77

Alliant Energy Powerhouse, 51

Amana Colonies Convention and Visitors Bureau, 115

Analog Vault, 128

Bart's Farm and Pumpkin Patch, 79

Bass Farms, 79

Big Grove Brewpub, 44–45

BIT Brewery, 7

Black Sheep Social Club, 34–35

Blooms Garden Center & Gift Shop, 122

Bloomsbury Farm, 87

Boston's, 22–23

Brewhemia, 36–37

Brucemore, 48, 57, 106–107

Brucemorchestra, 48

Café St. Pio, 36–37

Cappy's Pizzeria, 14–15

Caucho, 9

Cedar Lake, 70, 72

Cedar Rapids Freedom Festival, 56

Cedar Rapids Kernels, 83

Cedar Rapids Municipal Band, 57

Cedar Rapids Museum of Art, 65, 94, 95, 100

Cedar Rapids Opera Theater, 53

Cedar Rapids Public Library, 65, 97, 100

Cedar Rapids Roughriders, 82

Cedar Ridge Winery and Distillery, 5

Cedar River Garden Center, 122

Cedar Rock State Park, 112

Cedar Valley Nature Trail, 69

Cherry Building, The, 127

Cherry Hill Park, 81

Cherry Hill Pool, 81

City Square Park, 110

Class Act Restaurant, The, 28

Clock House Brewing, 7

Cobble Hill, 2, 9

Craft'd, 37

CSPS, 49

Czech Cottage, The, 131

Czech Village, 6, 34, 100, 130, 132

Dan and Debbie's Creamery, 12

Dash Coffee Roasters, 36–37

DOBRY Gift + Home, 131

Donutland, 13

Downtown Farmers Market, 123

Eastern Iowa Observatory, 60

Eat Shop, The, 44–45

El Super Burrito & Lupita's Bakery, 18

Feedwell Kitchen & Bakery, 32–33

Field of Dreams, 89

Five Seasons Ski Team, 54

Flying Wienie, The, 11

Fong's, 10

Found and Formed, 131

Frolics Village Boutique, 131

Frydae, 38–39

Funky Zebras, 131

Garden Wren Florist & Yarn, 131

General Store Pub, 43

Gilded Pear Gallery, 124

Giving Tree Theater, 58

Goldfinch Tap + Eatery, 38–39

Grant Wood Studio, 95

Greene Square Park, 65

Groundswell Café, 32–33

Hacienda Las Glorias, 19

Hawkeye Downs, 84

Herbert Hoover Presidential Library and Museum, 113

hip-stir, the, 38–39

History Center, The, 96

Hose House No. 4, 129

Hotel at Kirkwood Center, 28

Hotel Millwright, 115

House Divided Brewery, 7

Indian Creek Nature Center, 64

Iowa Brewing Company, 7

Iowa Ceramics Center and Glass Studio, 126

Irish Democrat, 16

Jazz Under the Stars, 57

Joensy's, 17

JOY, 120

Kava House & Café, 40

KCCK-FM, 57

Kismet Coffee & Bloom, 37

La Cantina Bar & Grill, 19

LA Trends Addict, 120

Leonardo's Restaurant & Pizza, 16

Lighthouse Inn and Supper Club, 42

Lightworks Café, 32–33

Lion Bridge Brewing Company, xvi, 6

Little Bohemia, 29

Lovely Bunches, 90

Lowe Park, 59

LP Street Food, 31

Lucita's Diner, 19

Luna Valley Farm, 24–25

Manchester Whitewater Park, 88

Marion, 15, 19, 37, 38–39, 58, 59, 77, 79, 110, 118–119, 120, 122

Marion Arts Festival, 110

McGrath Amphitheatre, 50

McLoud Run Stream, 72

Midtown Station, 23

Mini Pines Miniature Golf Course, 74

MODE, 120

Morgan Creek Park, 80

Moss Plant Shop, 122

Mount Trashmore, 67

Mount Vernon, 79, 86, 133

MOXIE + mortar, 44–45

Mr. Beans, 37

National Czech & Slovak Museum & Library, 104

Need Pizza, 14–15

NewBo City Market, 3, 41

New Pioneer Food Co-op, 73

Next Page Books, 128

Noelridge Greenhouses and Gardens, 71

Old MacDonald's Farm, 66

Orchestra Iowa, 48, 53

Palisades-Kepler State Park, 86

Paramount Theatre, 53

Persis Biryani Indian Grill, 27

Pheasant Run Farm, 90–91

Phong Lan Vietnamese Restaurant, 27

Pierson's Floral, 122

Pinicon Ridge Park, 78

Prairie Park Fishery, 68

Prairie Patch Farm, 85

Prairiewoods Franciscan Spirituality Center, 76

Promise & Blossom, 90

Quaker Oats, 102

Quarter Barrel, The, 7

RAYGUN, 125

R.G. Books, 20

rodina, 34–35

Roots in Bloom, 122

Rustic Hearth Bakery, 41

● ●

Sag Wagon, 70

SCOUT of Marion, 118

Scribe Stationer, 129

Seminole Valley Park, 108–109

Shakespeare Garden, 55

Short's Burgers & Shine, 38–39

Siamville Thai Cuisine, 27

Soko Outfitters, 132

Solon, 44–45

Stillwater Coffee Co., 36–37

Stone Wall Pizza, 25

Sutliff Farm and Cider House, 4

Sweet Mercantile Soda Fountain & Candy Shop, 131

Sykora Bakery, 8

Tee's Liberian Dish, 27

Theatre Cedar Rapids, 52

Third Base Brewery, 7

Tic Toc, 23

Tree of Five Seasons, 101

Tomaso's Pizza, 14–15

Twin Pines Golf Course, 74

Uptown Marion Artway, 111

Usher's Ferry Historic Village, 108

Veterans Memorial Building, 98

Villa's Patio, 19

Vino's Ristorante, 20

Vintage Market and Supply Co., 131

Vivian's Soul Food, 26

West End Shops and Diner, 119

Wickiup Hill Outdoor Learning Center, 75

Willie Ray's Q Shack, 21

Wilson's Orchard & Farm, 61

Zeppelins, 34–35

Zoey's, 14–15